Crisis Management

Is Social Media its new best friend
or its worst nightmare?

Robert A Clark

About The Author

Robert Clark is a Fellow of the Institute of Business Continuity Management and a Fellow of the British Computer Society. In addition to his many years of business continuity experience, he also has a Master's degree in Business Continuity, Security and Emergency Management awarded by Bucks New University. Robert's dissertation was entitled *"A Business Response to Terrorism"* and focused on Aviation Security and Tourism.

In 1973 he joined IBM as a computer operator. Big Blue was one of those forward thinking organisations that practiced business continuity management (BCM) before the expression had even been coined. But back in the 1970s, BCM was simply referred to as disaster recovery and was entirely focused on protecting the IT environment along with the associated electronic data.

It was less than twelve months into his 15 year IBM career that Robert first became exposed to BCM. Both local and overseas disaster fallback trials were regular features in the IBM calendar and often involved testing its recovery capability by transferring its UK IT operations to Germany or the Netherlands. Opportunities to rehearse Incident Management and Crisis Management techniques were frequent and became second nature. During his time with the corporation, the closest the operation came to a real disaster fallback was in 1974 during the UK miners' strike when power interruptions became commonplace.

His time with IBM was followed by a variety of positions including 11 years with Fujitsu Services (formerly ICL) working with clients on BCM related assignments. In 2005 he was tasked with validating Fujitsu's own BCM state of readiness across Europe. He has managed and delivered BCM solutions in the public sector, for large corporations, SMEs and central governments, gaining experience in several industries including banking, insurance, oil and gas, airline, manufacturing and retail across twelve different countries.

In 2014, his first book was published by IT Governance Publishing and was entitled "In Hindsight – a compendium of business continuity case studies" which got to Number One on the Amazon best sellers list.

He now splits his time between freelance Business Continuity consulting, writing and delivering BCM to both undergraduate and post graduate students at Manchester Metropolitan University. He has spent much of the last few years in Malta, where he has promoted BCM both through consultancy assignments and BCI licensed training.

As a member of Toastmasters International, Robert is no stranger to public speaking. An experienced keynote speaker, he promotes BCM whenever the opportunity presents itself.

Connect with the author on social media

Twitter: @BCMConsultancy
LinkedIn: maltabusinesscontinuity

Dedication

A chance exchange of messages via social media's LinkedIn platform between the author and Balvinder Singh Bains was the catalyst that spawned the idea for this book.

So many thanks Bal, this one's for you.

Other Books by the Author

"*I am constantly amazed by the number of executives who dismiss potential disasters as being too unlikely to consider, or who put off dealing with known risks because they have other things to worry about. This book is full of these people, and what happens in the case studies provides ample evidence to counter their complacency*"

Martin Caddick LLB MBA FBCI MIOR

"*If there exists a warm, friendly book about business continuity, then this is it. Reading this book is like having an elderly but very experienced uncle teaching you about the subject, sharing their experience, the lessons they have learned and (business continuity) war stories. It is an easy read, not overly complex, and is sprinkled with anecdotes and lessons learned from Bob's long career in ICT and business continuity*"

Charlie Maclean-Bristol FBCI FEPS

"*I thoroughly enjoyed reading Clark's book which is written in a style that makes it easy for anyone to understand without requiring a background in medicine or business. I have been involved in disaster management planning for the past ten years and yet I still found this book both enlightening and extremely informative*"

Dr Tanya Melillo MD, MSc(Dist), PhD
Head of Infectious Disease
Prevention and Control, MALTA

These books are available from Amazon in both Kindle and paperback format.

Foreword

We are living in what is often referred to as the information age during which time we have witnessed the global economy becoming ever more dependent upon Information Technology and the Internet. In making its own contribution to this digital revolution, since the first site was launched in the late 1990's social media has evolved at a breath taking pace. It has massively influenced just about every aspect of our lives and like the Internet it appears to be here to stay. There are naturally both advantages and disadvantages. While the benefits it brings on both a personal and commercial perspective are there to be enjoyed, it also has a darker side that individuals with evil intent have not been slow in exploiting.

In evaluating the case for social media being adopted as a crisis management communication channel, the author has considered both the rewards and drawbacks that this offers. It soon becomes clear to the reader that social media is capable of playing the 'hero' or the 'villain' in just about every crisis.

The broad spectrum of examples the author uses cover a number of industry sectors. He has successfully aligned these examples to many of the mainstream threats that organisations face on a daily basis. These include natural disasters, cyber threats, terrorism, adverse publicity, insider threat and even human error. He effectively demonstrates that a large corporation can just as easily find itself facing a major crisis in exactly the same way that a small or medium size enterprise can. Additionally, at both ends of the scale social media invariably finds some part to play.

Consideration is also given to social media's contribution to civil emergencies often when many hundreds or even thousands of vulnerable people can find themselves at risk. This book provides evidence that social media can and does help to save lives. Conversely, it can equally be held accountable for damaging our health both physically and psychologically.

I found the assessment of *Big Brother's* interest and involvement in social media fascinating. With skilful articulation social media's darker side is delineated highlighting what is certainly one of its extremely undesirable attributes. I was particularly captivated by a very realistic hypothesises that the text presents. It considers whether social media could have helped in savings more lives after the 9/11 Twin Towers attack had its capability back in 2001 been comparable to its modern day counterpart.

The style of writing is with an ease almost as if the author is chatting with you. The book is well researched and does not necessitate one to be an expert on either crisis management or social media to understand and appreciate the arguments presented. I have found this book to be an enlightening read with an excellent opportunity for learning more in this field.

So who should read this book? The obvious answer is anyone who has an interest in incident or crisis management in addition to media specialists. Individuals involved in law enforcement, emergency planning, risk management, business continuity and organisational resilience would also find this book a very useful source of reference. But is does not stop there. Just about anyone who uses social media personally or professionally would benefit from reading this book if only to fully understand the associated risks to their health and some cases even their careers.

I have known Robert Clark for over 10 years and I am very familiar with the other books he has written. Even though he has already reached the Number One position on the Amazon best sellers lists with his book "In Hindsight – a compendium of business continuity case studies", I firmly believe that this is his best work to date.

Catherine Feeney MSc FIH JP
Overseas Lecturer for Edinburgh Napier University

Preface

It started off as just an opportunity to speak at a seminar in the UK city of Leeds to an audience primarily drawn from the fire and rescue services and supporting industries. I had been invited to talk about crisis management and the role that social media was now playing as one of its communication channels. It felt as though I had been around crisis management for ever but of course social media was a comparatively new kid on the block with the first platform "Six Degrees" having been launched only as recently as 1997. It is not entirely clear exactly when the crisis management and social media first began courting each other but it is highly unlikely to have been before the arrival of the new millennium.

I had an abundance of relevant material that I could use but in preparing my presentation for the seminar my major challenge was not so much what to put in, but what to leave out. It left me thinking about what I could do with all the surplus material that time constraints dictated that I omitted from my slide set. The result was this book – my fourth publication to date. But as each day has passed that I spent writing, there has invariably been some kind of high profile social media story in the news that I could just not ignore. Consequently, as this book goes to publication, some of the examples and case studies that I have used are literally hot off the press.

Through my own use of social media both personally and professionally, my business continuity consultancy work and my academic research I was well aware of the good, the bad and the ugly sides of social media. Yes social media can be a force for good and certainly provides enormous benefit as a communication channel for crisis management. But it can also appear to be its nemesis by creating what sometimes seems to be as many if not more crises than it helps resolve.

We need to recognise that social media is far from perfect and its ugly or dark side is certainly nothing to eulogise about. In reality it is perhaps far worse than many people realise. You will you come across references to it facilitating the despicable practices of trolling, cyber-bullying, sexting and grooming. Moreover, this book also provides an example of terrorists using social media to provide a live running commentary while they committed their acts of atrocity. Via social media I also personally witnessed an active shooter attack unfolding at a school in which students caught up in the incident were posting videos onto Twitter of what was happening.

Not one to miss an opportunity, 'Big Brother' has also managed to grab a piece of the action. One entire chapter has been devoted exclusively to the subject of state surveillance and censorship. In fact, people have been imprisoned for criminal offences having been convicted based on the evidence that social media has furnished. Moreover, planned terrorist activities have also been thwarted as the result of social media intercepts by security services.

Social media also comes in for criticism for the primarily negative effect that it is having on the education sector. Moreover and rather worryingly, there are also the early warning signs of its potential health threat legacy – both physical and psychological. There is now a disease that has been named after one of the social media platforms called 'WhatAppItis'. Such is the associated concern in health circles

that it has even been featured in the leading medical journal –
The Lancet. But not all is gloom and doom out there in social
media land as, despite the growing concerns surrounding the
health issues, there is definite evidence that social media has a
growing reputation for actually helping to save lives.

Finally, no account of social media would be complete without
mention of fake news. Since his rise to political prominence
Donald Trump has significantly raised the profile of fake news
and not without some justification. Regardless of their motives,
those who wish to peddle sensationalism through fabricated
news stories have found the perfect conduit in social media.

So whatever your own definition of a crisis happens to be,
whether it is personal or professional, I would like to think that
somewhere in this book you will invariably find examples that
will resonate with you.

Table of Contents

About The Author...iii

Dedication v

Other Books by the Author vi

Foreword..viii

Preface xi

Table of Contents xiv

Table of Figures xviii

1   Introduction 1

2   Social Media Overview..6

3   What Constitutes a Crisis? 12

   3.1   Preparing for crises 18

   3.2   Creating your Crisis Communication Plan 24

      3.2.1   Pro-active social media monitoring 25

      3.2.2   When should you activate crisis management.............27

      3.2.3   Reactive crisis management mode 28

      3.2.4   Tips on Engagement....................................35

      3.2.5   When is your crisis management desk open? 37

4   The best of friends or worst of enemies? 38

   4.1   United screw-up in full view of the world 38

   4.2   Virgin Trains strike the right balance..................47

   4.3   Al Shabaab live-tweet terrorist attack................50

4.4   Can Social Media Cause a PR Crisis 52

4.4.1   Inflammatory personal view tweeted on company's Twitter account 53

4.4.2   Getting a bad TripAdvisor review scares me 55

4.4.3   The tale of two banks 57

4.5   Don't Let Communications Become the Crisis 60

4.6   The Insider Threat 63

4.7   Hacked twitter account displays rival logo 65

4.8   Carry on marketing regardless ? 67

4.9   Mustard lovers close ranks 71

4.10   Who'd be a soccer referee? 72

4.11   Prison sentences for social media trolls 76

4.12   Fake News 78

4.12.1   The Man Who Never Was 79

4.12.2   Arsenal invest £36 Million in teenage soccer sensation 80

4.12.3   The 2016 US Presidential Election 81

4.12.4   That green liquid contains cyanide, doesn't it? 86

4.12.5   Fake blood appeal after 2017 Manchester bombing 88

4.13   Crowd funding after Manchester bombing 88

4.14   Has social media saved lives? 89

4.14.1   Kenya Red Cross 89

4.14.2   Hurricane Harvey - 2017 90

4.14.3 Stranded Indian workers faced starvation....................94

4.14.4 Just to let you know, I'm safe !......................................95

4.14.5 Injured biker rescued by Twitter.................................96

4.14.6 Kawasaki disease diagnosed on Facebook.................97

4.14.7 Sadly social media couldn't help this time...................98

4.15 We are all human...99

4.15.1 A *'plane'* mistake to make...99

4.15.2 Whoops – "Wrong button" says Minister..................101

4.15.3 Take cover - Incoming !!...102

4.16 Is social media having its very own crisis?...................102

5 Massive negative impact seen in education............................104

5.1 Social Media disrupts the classroom............................106

5.2 Would adding social media to the curriculum help?..........110

5.3 Threats of violence at schools including shootings............115

5.4 When will it end?...117

6 Is *'Big Brother'* watching us on social media too?.....................121

6.1 Social media intercept prevents terrorist attack.................124

6.2 China censors Hong Kong's 'Umbrella Revolution'...........126

6.3 Social media helps convict hundreds of UK rioters...........128

6.4 Police use social media metadata to track individuals.......131

6.5 Witness for the Prosecution and the Defence...................132

6.6 Is big business now the new Big Brother?...........................135

7 Could social media have made any difference? 137

  7.1 The Piper Alpha Disaster 137

  7.2 Terrorism, 9/11 and the Twin Towers 139

    7.2.1 The potential benefits from social media....................149

    7.2.2 The negative aspects of using social media 151

8 On a more personal note...... 156

  8.1 Can social media damage your health?............................156

  8.2 Emotions to the fore 160

  8.3 Social media can inhibit your career 161

9 Conclusion 167

10 Do you want to become a best-selling author 171

11 Review Request 172

12 Other Books by the Author..173

13 Glossary of Terms 175

14 Works Cited...181

15. Open Government License 207

Table of Figures

Figure 1: List of Social Media Platforms..8

Figure 2: Selection of complaints about #Whirlpool............................10

Figure 3: Examples of crisis creating events......................................16

Figure 4: Examples of local, country, regional and global crises 17

Figure 5: UK National Risk Register - impact & probability matrix 21

Figure 6: UK NRR risk legend for hazards, disease, accidents and societal risks..22

Figure 7: Southwest Airlines - standby for more information...............33

Figure 8: One of many positive responding tweets 34

Figure 9: United CEO Twitter response to United Flight 3411 42

Figure 10: @VirginTrains tweet re: incident at Hemel Hempstead 49

Figure 11: Offensive tweet about Barack Obama's grandmother 55

Figure 12: Facebook apology issued by KitchenAid 56

Figure 13: Peston and Franchi comparison of traditional and social media influence (2015)..60

Figure 14: Tweet by passenger escaping from crashed aircraft 61

Figure 15: Asiana Airlines Facebook post...63

Figure 16: McDonald's anti-Trump hacked tweet...............................68

Figure 17: Typical response to Adidas Boston Marathon email..........70

Figure 18: TripAdvisor suspends Café Rossetti's profile....................76

Figure 19: £36 million spent on teenage soccer sensation 81

Figure 20: Crowd size comparisons at Obama's and Trumps inaugurations 86

Figure 21: Texas citizens instructed not to use social media 94

Figure 22: Sushma Swaraj's Twitter commitment 95

Figure 23: BA accidentally shares Virgin Atlantic's posting................101

Figure 24: Minister presses wrong button 102

Figure 25: World Trade Centre map – prior to 9/11 attack.................148

1 Introduction

Having to face and manage a crisis is nothing new. Organisations in the private and public sectors along with NGO's such as *'The International Red Cross and Red Crescent'* and *'Medicins sans Frontieres'* have been doing this for countless years. Consequently it is not the intention of this book to provide instruction on how to manage a crisis. Instead, it examines the comparatively new and, what I consider to be, unholy alliance that crisis management has forged with social media by adopting it as an additional communication channel. This arrangement may seem to be a logical progression vis-à-vis the managing of crisis communications. Although multi-faceted, social media has essentially turned crisis management into a spectator sport that just about anyone with Internet access and a smart phone can watch and, if they feel so inclined, even join in. The case studies in this book will reveal just how much of a double edged sword social media can be while demonstrating how its relationship with crisis management can often be antagonistic.

A vital aspect of effectively managing a crisis has always been the ability to communicate with an organisation's stakeholders and when necessary this needs to be a two-way dialogue. In addition to word of mouth, for centuries the only means of communicating in a crisis was by using the hand written or the printed word. Signalling methods such as Semaphore provided an alternative but it had inherent shortcomings insofar as the message recipient had to be in sight of the sender at all times. Even so, Napoleonic semaphore was the world's first telegraph network, carrying messages across 19th Century France faster than ever before. A chain of semaphore towers equipped with pivoting shutters was built for transmitting messages over long distances.

But in bygone years, it took as long as it took for information to disseminate – in some cases it would have taken weeks or even months to cross the globe. In the case of the 1805 British naval victory at the Battle of Trafalgar, it took more than two weeks for the news to reach the Admiralty in London, a distance of less than 1,500 miles (2,350 km).

During the late 19th and early 20th century more efficient means of communicating were developed. By the start of World War I much of the globe was connected by submarine telegraph cables around 80% of which was controlled by the British. This had for example reduced the time taken for communications between the UK and Australia from 3 months to 7 hours. It was 1876 when the telephone was invented even so, it took 75 years before it reached its first 50 million users, 38 years for the radio, 13 years for television, 4 years for the Internet and 1.5 years for arguably the best known social media platform, Facebook, to achieve the same milestone.

Source: Aeppel, 2015

However, as of the second quarter of 2017, Facebook claimed it had two billion monthly active users - circa 26% of the entire population of the planet.

Today data can circumnavigate the globe in a matter of seconds and with the advance in technology expectations of immediate availability of information has evolved. In fact as far back as the 1991 Gulf War, television crews were often able to transmit live images of cruise missiles hitting their targets in Baghdad. For the first time generals had been afforded the ability to watch a battle in progress on a monitor in real time.

Social media has been around since 1997 when the first platform "Six Degrees" was introduced. This book looks at how social media, like radio, television and telephone before it, has provided organisations with an additional and very effective communication channel. By providing another channel, it reduces the dependency on the more traditional means of communication but it does not replace those channels.

Many organisations have now embraced various social media platforms for marketing purposes. However, through a series of case studies, the main focus will not just be on its recognition as a communication channel by crisis managers, but also to examine the dangers of failing to take it seriously when a crisis strikes.

In the short time that social media had been available, it has changed the face of crisis management. Complaints maybe once considered trivial by suppliers can now take on a mantle of importance. In fact, it just takes one irate customer's complaint magnified by the power of social media to mobilise support akin to rabble rousing as a single voice can be joined by many others. The example of Dr Dao being physically dragged off a United Airlines flight is a point in case and will be examined later in the book in section 4.1.

There are over forty social media related incidents covered in this book and the examples included are from a very 'broad church'. Consequently they are comprised of a wide variety of illustrations of how social media can be both a force for good and evil in the way it has affected individuals, small and medium size businesses, large billion dollar corporations and even countries.

The book also looks at social media's contribution in saving lives that have been threatened by crises of varying magnitude – sometimes it was just individuals, while on other occasions hundreds and maybe even thousands owe their lives to its existence. There are those who believe that social media is causing a crisis in education and an examination is undertaken of both the positive but mainly negative effects that it is having in the classroom. Evidence is provided on some of the legal aspects of Social Media's misuse and abuse including details of convictions and subsequent incarcerations that followed. One chapter presents a hypothesis that considers whether the availability of social media may have had an influence on the number of people to have survived the 9/11 attack on the World Trade Centre Twin Towers. Another chapter has been dedicated to investigating how Big Brother is taking full advantage of social media and how the phenomenon seems to be introducing a culture of self-policing amongst parts of its user community. There have been several ways identified in which social media can damage your health – both physically and psychologically. Evidence has also been presented regarding the damage it can do to your career. Finally, no book of this nature would be complete without considering the issue of 'Fake News' along with social media's own contribution to the topic.

In thinking of social media as a communication channel for crisis management, we must remember that one size does not fit all. For example, the approach for dealing with a product failure or recall may need to differ from say an insider threat or adverse publicity. As an organisation you may find yourself initially on the back foot and having to apologise possibly even for a situation that was not of your making. Alternatively, when it comes to life threatening scenarios such as a plane crash or terrorist attack, certainly in the first instance people will need information and direction rather than apologies - recriminations may come later.

In summary, through the pages of this book, the case is presented for the essential inclusion of social media within organisational crisis management communication plans.

2   Social Media Overview

"Social media is not a conversation. It is where a conversation takes place" – Jay Baer, Social Media Strategist

Social media is a generic phrase that we use to describe what businesses and individuals post on websites and apps such as Facebook, Twitter, Instagram, Snapchat, Pinterest, LinkedIn and YouTube et al. It provides us with the means to communicate via a computer, tablet or smart phone, share photographs, videos and experiences. Social media also affords the opportunity for individuals to build their own persona and to showcase their talents, something also not lost on recruiters and head-hunters. There is of course no limit on how many social media platforms that individuals or organisations can be active on although this will invariably be constrained by the time available to manage these accounts. Personally, I am active on only six - Facebook, LinkedIn, YouTube, Twitter, TripAdvisor and Skype and I use these platforms for a mixture of personal and business use.

"There is no way organisations can hold back the flow of social media, so it is better to put policies and technologies in place to manage it" - David Cripps, Information Security Officer at Investec (Ashford, 2013)

Businesses are increasingly using social media for marketing purposes as it enables them to build relationships, increase their visibility and promote their services and products. But unlike any previous time in history, social media has also empowered consumers who have found that they are no longer a lone voice in the wilderness. If they have a complaint with a supplier, social media provides them with the platform to not only air their grievance but also find other individuals who may have a similar issue. Moreover, it allows anyone the opportunity to share what they are passionate about and find an audience of like-minded people almost anywhere around the world. Furthermore, the ubiquity of the smartphone has created the wherewithal to disseminate information to a worldwide audience in real-time.

The first recognizable social media site, Six Degrees, was launched in 1997. The instant messaging service Skype arrived in 2003, Facebook in 2004 and Twitter in 2006. As of 2017 there were over two hundred social media platforms listed excluding those specifically intended for users in mainland China such as Weibo, WeChat and RenRen. That said it is not the intent to analyse and compare the multitude of platforms that exist today but to consider how collectively they are influencing crisis management – for better and for worse. However, to fully explore the case studies included in this book it has been necessary to cite specific social media platforms and their involvement in the examples being assessed.

There is no doubt that Facebook has become the most popular social media platform. The original pioneer, Six Degrees, was like a crude version of Facebook, allowing users to link up with friends and family etc. Not all social media ventures been successful and some have long since disappeared including Six Degrees. In the following table is a categorisation of the social media platforms as defined by Hootsuite an organisation that describes itself as:

"Not just a social relationship platform or just a tech company. We are creators, innovators, and builders dedicated to revolutionizing the way you communicate" - (Hootsuite, 2018)

LIST OF SOCIAL MEDIA PLATFORMS	
PLATFORM	PURPOSE
Social networks	Connect with people
Media sharing networks	Share photos, videos, and other media
Discussion forums	Share news and ideas
Bookmarking and content curation networks	Discover, save, and share new content
Consumer review networks	Find and review businesses
Blogging and publishing networks	Publish content online
Interest-based networks	Share interests and hobbies
Social shopping networks	Shop online
Sharing economy networks	Trade goods and services
Anonymous social networks	Communicate anonymously

Figure 1: List of Social Media Platforms
Source: (Hootsuite, 2018)

It should be possible to pigeon hole each social media site into one of these categories although some like Facebook can be placed into multiple categories.

When I was writing this chapter, I took a look at the BBC website's business page to see who was moaning about which organisations and why. I came across a number of reports about problems with Whirlpool products in addition to an admission from Whirlpool itself that:

> *"A million potentially deadly tumble dryers could still be being used in British homes" - (Read, 2017)*

This reminded of the story I had heard a year or two before concerning tumble dryers catching fire. It appears that in the time that had passed since the story first broke, Whirlpool had only managed to repair about 50% of the faulty machines in the UK.

As a matter of course, organisations should be actively monitoring social media for any potentially damaging posts regarding the organisation itself, its staff, products and services etc. For example, by entering a hashtag '#' in front of a search for a brand name can reveal what is currently being talked about in relation to the brand. So by entering #whirlpool, I took a look at what was being said on social media about the organisation. The illustration that follows is just a brief snapshot of the many comments I came across on Twitter. One of the complainants, Paola C, actually tweeted in both English and then again in Spanish.

Tim
@007TW8

Do not purchase @whirlpoolusa appliances. You will regret it if there's ever a problem. Their customer service is nonexistent. #whirlpool

5:51 AM - 20 Oct 2017

♡ 1   ⟲   ♡   ✉

Tweet your reply

Whirlpool Care ● @WhirlpoolCare · 20 Oct 2017   ⌄
Replying to @007TW8
We're very sorry to hear this. Please DM your contact info along with model/serial #. We'd be happy to look into this for you.

♡   ⟲   ♡   ✉

Adam Belcher
@Bwortang

Did anyone else replace their tumble dryer last year after safety risks, only for the new one to then die? #whirlpool #hotpoint

11:25 PM - 26 Oct 2017 from Salisbury, England

2 Retweets 3 Likes

♡ 3   ⟲ 2   ♡ 3   ✉

10

Paola C
@pao0879

Follow ⌄

#Whirlpool
Worst service ever. I waited for technical support for repair 4 times, they never came. Your supervisor was rude @WhirlpoolCare

7:28 PM - 25 Oct 2017

1 Like

💬 1   ⇄   ♡ 1   ✉

Figure 2: Selection of complaints about #Whirlpool
Source: Twitter

In January 2017, a little over a year after the origin story broke, the consumer magazine 'Which' posted an article on its website that criticised Whirlpool's handling of the tumble dryer issues as a "slow and poor service". It added that *Whirlpool was still failing its consumers*" (Which, 2017).

What I find ironical is the way in which Whirlpool's share price has behaved since the story first broke on Monday 23rd November 2015 as it seems to bare no relation to the torrid time the organisations has been experiencing with its products. Having closed on the previous Friday at $162.27 within a week it had risen over $5 to $167.29. As I write it has climbed to over $182 which in no way reflects the mood of its consumers being expressed via the media (NYSE, 2018).

3 What Constitutes a Crisis?

It is perhaps worth noting that the availability of guidance from relevant crisis management standards has been a fairly recent event. In 2014, the British Standard 11200:2014 replaced its Publicly Available Specification (PAS) predecessor, the 2011 published PAS 200. Given the history between British Standards and the International Standards (ISO), it is highly likely that BS 11200:2014 will be adopted by the latter at some future point.

> *"The Standard (BS 11200:2014) focuses on how to manage a crisis, which is defined as 'an abnormal and unstable situation that threatens the organisation's strategic objectives, reputation or viability', as opposed to 'lower level' incidents that have a different set of characteristics"* - (Cockram, 2015)

Crisis is a word that can be used rather liberally. If you ask ten CEO's to give you an example of what they consider to be a crisis, you will quite possibly get ten different answers. Variations in the responses can also be driven by the size of the organisations and the nature of their respective business. As a consultant, I have often asked CEO's what threats to their respective businesses keep them awake at night. Like the definition for a 'crisis' the answers can be varied.

Cockram's summary above of BS 11200's crisis definition implies that the scope relates to a single organisation. So let's put some context on what this book considers it to be. On the one hand a crisis can be of a personal nature which in recent times some people choose to play out using social media. However, from a more organisational perspective, I have always considered a crisis to be an adverse event or series of events that causes extensive disruption perhaps to an individual organisation, a town, a country or, indeed, in a worst case scenario, to the entire world. Fortunately the latter does not happen very often although a good example of such circumstances would be the Spanish Influenza pandemic of 1918 which killed an estimated 50 million people worldwide.

Today one impending global crisis which is rarely out of the news is of course the threat of climate change and there is no shortage of posts to be found on social media addressing the issue. We are already seeing some early warning signs (e.g. an increase in drought, heat waves, flooding, wildfires, shrinking ice caps and glaciers etc.) But despite the Paris Accord, all the rhetoric and formulation of action plans, I for one still sense a lack of urgency. I liken it to a scenario where you have stalled your car on a railway crossing and in the distance you can see an express train charging towards you. If you can get the car started or push it off the crossing before the train arrives, you can avoid what would otherwise be an inevitable disaster.

There are those individuals who argue fervently that climate change is not only real but is the consequence of man's mismanagement of the environment. Others believe it to be a quirk of nature claiming that weather patterns are cyclic and the changes we are witnessing are in line with that recurrent activity. Finally there is that group of individuals who are in complete denial that the phenomenon is actually happening at all. Whatever your own personal view of the situation happens to be, let us live in hope that the legacy we leave our descendants will be a positive one and what action is being taken to address climate change is not too little – too late.

Many of the crises featured in this book are man-made although, on a country, regional and even global scale Mother Nature will frequently have a hand in creating some of the most challenging crises that mankind is called upon to deal with. While this list not definitive, these will typically include the likes of pandemics, volcanic eruptions, earthquakes, tsunamis, adverse weather, floods, droughts and wildfires etc. Moreover, there is never a timetable of forthcoming natural disasters published so we might be better prepared.

But we are improving in terms of understanding and occasionally pre-empting these natural phenomena. Examples include, the spread of contagions that have the potential to evolve into pandemics, forecasting volcanic eruptions and more accurate weather predictions. In 2017 scientists were able to warn that in Bali the Mount Agung volcano was threatening to erupt and in the Caribbean area hurricane warnings for Harvey and Irma were issued several days before they made landfall. In each of these cases sufficient time was available to evacuate people located in vulnerable areas. Moreover, while we cannot stop the inevitable, we are seeing social media playing its part in helping to manage the humanitarian crises that frequently accompany these natural disasters.

Figure 3 provides a few examples of the type of crises that can occur at a local or organisational level right through to global scenarios. It is plausible these crises can be upgraded from say a regional level to a global level. Had the 2013 Ebola epidemic in West Africa spread to other continents, the World Health

Organisation would almost certainly have upgraded it to a global pandemic. Conversely, a crisis can be downgraded too. Staying with the clinical theme, Smallpox was once a global threat but by the late 1970's cases were only being reported in Africa meaning it had become a regional problem before being officially declared eradicated in 1980. Figure 4 identifies some specific examples of crises that have occurred in recent times.

GLOBAL	Pandemics (e.g. SARS, Influenza, HIV / AIDS etc.) Global Recession Currency fluctuations Oil crisis
REGIONAL	Epidemic (e.g. Ebola, MERS, etc.) Hurricanes Tsunamls Volcanic ash clouds Drought
COUNTRY	Wars Civil unrest Terrorism Earthquakes Economic / political disruption
LOCAL	Fires Floods Adverse media coverage Loss of expertise Industrial action ICT failure / Cyber attack

Figure 3: Examples of crisis creating events

Threat Type	Event
Wars, Riots, Protests, Civil Unrest	• War in Croatia and Slovenia in 1991 • Arab Spring and Syrian civil war 2010 onward • Hong Kong Occupy Central 2014 • Unrest in Northern Ireland 1968-98
Environmental	• Indian Ocean tsunami in 2004 • Icelandic volcano Eyjafjallajökull's ash cloud 2010 • Hurricanes Irma and Harvey 2017 • Earthquake in Haiti in 2010 • Sahelian drought 1980's onward
Disease (Pandemics, Epidemics etc.)	• SARS in 2002-2003 • Ebola in 2014 • Foot and Mouth 2001 • Zika virus in 2016
Terrorism	• 9/11 World Trade Centre Twin Towers attack 2001 • 7/7 London Tube and bus bombings 2005 • Paris bombing and shooting attacks 2015 and 2016 • Berlin Christmas market attack 2016 • Manchester Arena bombing 2017
Transport	• Costa Concordia cruise ship capsized 2012 • Malaysian Airlines flight MH370 2014 disappearance • Germanwings suspected pilot suicide 2015 • British Airways ICT Failure 2017
Political, Economic	• Asian financial crisis 1997 • Middle East – ongoing, Iran • International Great Recession 2007–09+ • Brexit and the plummeting value of the Pound
Physical	• Fire at the Windsor Tower, Madrid 2005 • European Flooding 2013 • Manchester city centre exclusion zone 1996 (6 months) • Worldcom and Enron fraudulent accounting 2001 • Brexit causing potential resource shortages in UK 2018

Figure 4: Examples of local, country, regional and global crises

3.1 Preparing for crises

It is quite commonplace to find international bodies like the World Health Organisation (WHO), as well most countries and large corporations right through to Small and Medium size Enterprises (SME's) making some form of preparation to better deal with whatever crises that may come their way. Thinking back to Figure 3 and Figure 4, there is a variety of threats to consider right from a local through to a global level. Even so, these threats do not represent a definitive list and there will be others that organisations will need to consider. Regardless of where an organisation fits into the overall scheme of things (e.g. large global player, small local enterprise, one man band etc.) they should analyse the threats they are facing and produce a risk assessment. But some people are not sure of the difference between a threat and a risk while others erroneously use the words interchangeably so here is a simple explanation:

If someone said to you "I think it might rain today" – that is a threat. However if that person had said "there is a 70% chance of rain today and this morning the television weather presenter predicted that we could expect as much as 2 inches (50 mm) rainfall" – well that is a risk. What's the difference? Simply that a risk has an associated probability of occurring and a likely impact if it does occur while a threat does not.

The WHO has what it refers to as a war plan which is a global action plan that would be used in the event of a pandemic being declared. In fact this plan was activated when the Severe Acute Respiratory Syndrome (SARS) began to spread rapidly in 2003. Like many countries, the UK publishes an updated version of its National Risk Register of civil emergencies (UK NRR) every two or three years. In 2012, it also published a document called Smart Tips for Category 1 Responders Using Social Media in Emergency Management. Despite the title and being published six years before this book, the Smart Tips document contains information that could be useful to organisations setting up their social media communications for their crisis management. Both of these documents are in the public domain and can be downloaded from the Internet.

As previously mentioned, one size does not fit all and a comparison of a cross section of national risk registers would certainly help to illustrate this point by demonstrating the diversity of different risks that countries face. However, there is one risk in particular flagged by the UK NRR that is worthy of note primarily because it has been consistently referred to by every national risk register that I have personally come across. That is a pandemic. The UK's risk assessment process has estimated that the probability of a severe pandemic occurring within the next five years is between 1-in-20 and 1-in-2 while its projected impact is expected to be catastrophic which is the highest impact rating. Note that we are referring to the risk of a pandemic and not the threat of a pandemic because there is an associated probability and impact.

The contagion is expected to be influenza, probably avian flu, but there are a number of other nasty novel contagions out there that should not be ruled out. If this risk becomes a reality it is estimated that up to half the UK population could be infected and as many as 750,000 fatalities (circa 1.1% of the population). Such a scenario would result in a global cataclysm and by transposing the UK's estimates onto a global scale; there could be as many as 100 million fatalities worldwide.

In reviewing the UK's pandemic probability and impact assessments, it is not difficult to understand the potential scale of such a catastrophe. In my book entitled "Business Continuity and the Pandemic Threat", I looked at the issue from a global, national, organisational and even an individual perspective. We will not be able to prevent a pandemic from happening but we can prepare ourselves for what history tells us is inevitable.

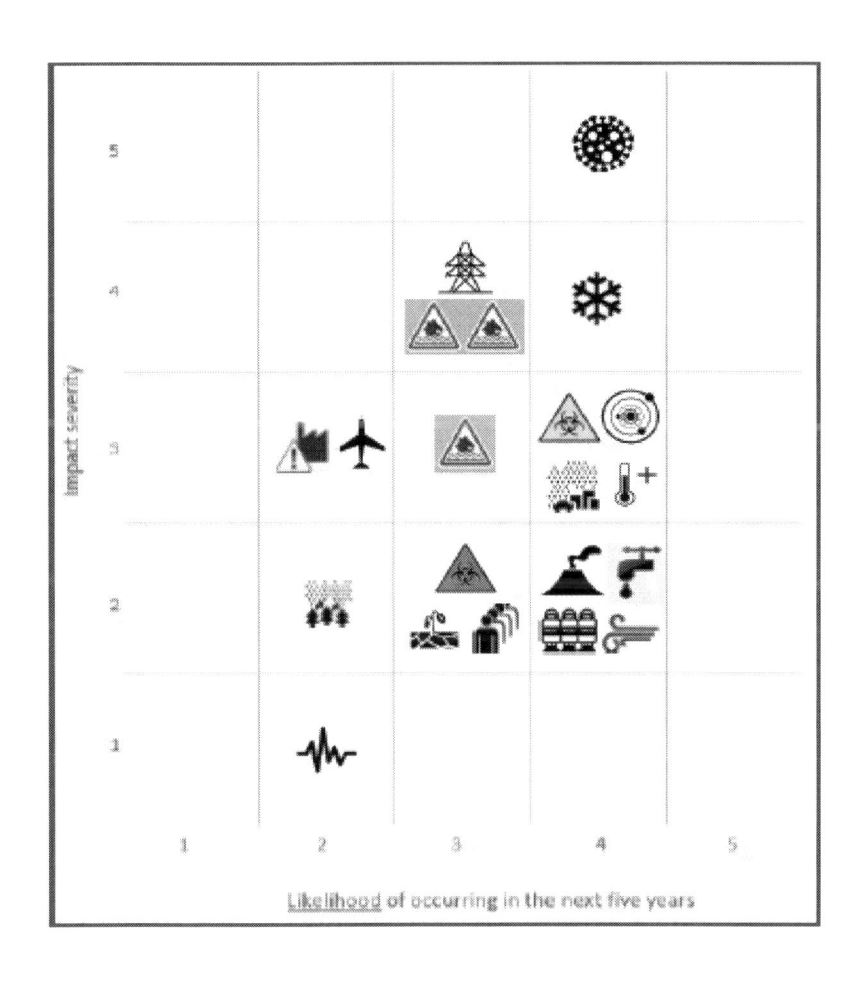

Figure 5: UK National Risk Register - impact & probability matrix
Source: (UK Cabinet Office, 2017)

KEY

Natural hazards

- Coastal flooding
- River flooding
- Surface water flooding
- Storms and gales
- Cold and snow
- Heatwave
- Drought
- Space weather
- Volcanic eruptions
- Poor air quality
- Earthquakes
- Wildfires

Diseases

- Pandemic influenza
- Emerging infectious disease
- Animal disease

Major accidents

- Widespread electricity failure
- Transport accidents
- Industrial and urban accidents
- System failures

Societal risks

- Industrial action
- Public disorder

Figure 6: UK NRR risk legend for hazards, disease, accidents and societal risks

Source: (UK Cabinet Office, 2017)

The illustration in Figure 5 is an extract from the UK NRR and depicts one of the two risk assessment matrices. This one deals with hazards, disease, accidents and societal risks while a second matrix (not included in this book) deals with malicious attacks such as terrorism and cyber-attacks. Across both matrices, there is only one risk that has been given an impact rating of '5' and that is a pandemic.

If a severe pandemic does occur, we can only guess what affect it will have on social media. Yes, there will lots of information (and unfortunately misinformation) posted on the various social media platforms. Although the SARS virus was contained, there was little that could prevent the regular and alarming cable television news reports while many bloggers peddled unfounded and startling conspiracy theories. To get some idea of how the general public might take to social media we need only look at lessons taken from that SARS outbreak of 2002-3. During the period February 8th to 10th 2003 the SMS text message:

'There is a fatal flu in Guangzhou'

was sent 126 million times just from mobile phones in the city of Guangzhou alone (Brahmbhatt & Dutta, 2008). At the time of the SARS outbreak, this southern Chinese city of Guangzhou (formerly known as Canton) had a population of around 14 million inhabitants. Yet to reiterate, over a two day period that one text message warning was sent 126 million times. That has the potential to translate into astronomical numbers in terms of Twitter and Facebook posts including any subsequent retweeting and sharing when you extrapolate the potential effect on a global scale.

For more information about pandemics and the SARS outbreak there was a video posted on YouTube in 2012 by TED-Ed called "How pandemics spread" which you may find informative.

There is one erratum item to bring to your attention with regard to this video. It mentioned that in the few months of the SARS crisis, the cost to the global economy was US$10 billion. However, this figure has been subsequently revised upwards and was closer to US$50 billion with around 3 million jobs lost in from the tourism industry alone (Feeney, 2014).

3.2 Creating your Crisis Communication Plan

"Having a company-wide plan in place will empower you to act quickly and effectively when a crisis begins. Instead of wasting time debating how to handle things on social media, you'll be empowered to take action and prevent the crisis from growing out of control" - *(Dawley, 2016)*

You cannot be effective in a crisis without a communication plan especially as the existence of social media means that information can now circumnavigate the globe in seconds. However if your organisation has not developed its communication plan, using social media as part of your crisis management strategy is probably not going to help you. So whether you are developing a new plan or updating an existing plan to incorporate social media, there are a number of tasks you will need to undertake before your plan is good to go. That said, some organisations choose to employ a specialist public relations companies for some or even all of their crisis communications.

In Chapter 1, I explained that the intent of this book was not to instruct on how to manage a crisis. Likewise, as this book's primary focus is on crisis management and its relationship with social media, first and foremost this chapter considers the actions that need to be taken to incorporate social media into an existing communications plan. It is not intended to replace any other old and established means of crisis communications channels but rather to complement them.

From a social media perspective, ideally the plan should be divided into two parts – proactive and the reactive. Section 3.1 provided an insight in to the various threats that an organisation can expect to face and in the remainder of this chapter we will look at the part that social media will be expected to play. However, we must not lose sight of the fact that some crisis scenarios could actually be caused by social media itself which begs the question *'is social media a poacher, a gamekeeper or both*?'

3.2.1 Pro-active social media monitoring

This pro-active part would be a business-as-usual set of activities dealing with the ongoing monitoring of media channels and in particular social media. It would have the objective of detecting and monitoring any references to the organisation including any mention of its products and services or staff etc. As part of their brief, your team should be analysing social media traffic for relevant emerging issues along with potential problems ideally while they are still in their embryonic stages. In the event that something derogatory or detrimental to the organisation's interests is detected, you may choose to switch from pro-active to reactive mode. Likewise if some kind of serious incident occurs that is likely to generate high levels of interest in the organisation, again switch to reactive mode. As you will see from the case studies later in the book it is also a sensible move to stop marketing activities when you activate your crisis management mode.

To assist with the passive monitoring there are a number of organisations in the marketplace such as Google Alerts, Hootsuite, BuzzSumo and Zoho Social that offer tools help with the monitoring. If you choose to go down this route always ensure that you understand your requirements before evaluating and selecting one of these tools otherwise you may find that you end up with a solution chasing a problem.

With or without a tool to help, you should be monitoring specific key words and hashtags (#) that will enable you to better protect your brand and reputation from any potentially damaging social media traffic. For example you should be monitoring for:

1. Your company's or organisation's name including any generally recognised abbreviations (e.g. British Airways + BA and GlaxoSmithKline + GSK etc.)
2. All of your products, services and brands
3. The names of your C-Suite (e.g. CEO, CFO, CIO etc.) including the Chairman and all board members. It is not beyond the realms of possibility that one of them could do or say something that reflects badly on your organisation.
4. The names of all other public facing members of staff
5. All enquiries, comments and complaints coming through your Customer Services department
6. Influencers that operate within your sphere of interest
7. Keywords related to your industry

8. Watch your competition as their crises could reflect negatively on the industry as whole. This may also present itself as an opportunity for your organisation.
9. Monitor your key suppliers for early warning of a potential upstream supply chain failures
10. Watch your principal clients for early warning of a potential downstream supply chain failures

3.2.2 When should you activate crisis management

So when exactly should you switch from passive monitoring into crisis management mode will actually be a matter for your organisation to decide. There is more than one answer to this question although the obvious one is when a serious incident occurs that has the potential to have a detrimental effect on your organisation. It is quite possible that you know about it before it registers on social media's radar. However, as you will see from the examples included in in Chapter 4, you cannot assume that this will always be the case.

The inventory of possible incidents can be extensive and could include fire, flood, terrorism, cyber-attack, insider threat and earthquake. The list goes on. But if your organisation has completed a threat analysis exercise and produced its corresponding risk assessment (see section 3.1) then you should have covered off most of the threats you are facing. Social media specialists Hootsuite recommend that you should consider the following type of approach, looking at your thresholds to determine your next steps:

- **Less than five negative mentions per hour:** Continue monitoring closely. Compile a report for senior management to review at the end of the day.

- **More than five negative mentions per hour:** bring management's attention to the increase in negative traffic

- **More than 10 negative mentions per hour, for more than three consecutive hours:** begin officially rolling out the crisis management communication plan including the social media aspect.

Source: (Dawley, 2016)

3.2.3 Reactive crisis management mode

Social media teams who may be usually focused on content management for marketing purposes may need to be retrained so they can be redeployed onto crisis management as the need arises. So in preparing for switching to the reactive mode of crisis management communications, your plan should consider the 'who', the 'how' and the 'what'.

- **Who** do we need to communicate with (aka our stakeholders)
- **How** are you going to communicate with them? It is possible that if the crisis you are dealing with disrupts some of your communications channels in which case you will need to have contingency plans in place that identifies alternative channels to use. To that end, it is better to identify alternative means of communication before a crisis kicks-off rather than have to consider other options after a disruption has occurred.

- Finally, **what** are we going to tell them and also remember conversations may need to be two-way?

You will also need to be clear about who is responsible for each communication related task and identify appropriate backups. It is essential to decide upon spokesperson and ensure they are trained in advance. It is also entirely possible that the spokesperson who is expected to deal with the more traditional media is not the same person who represents the organisation via social media. You may conclude that because of their prominent position in the organisation the CEO is the right person to speak to Television, Radio and Press while someone else is responsible for social media. However, a word of warning – the head of the organisation may seem the obvious choice but they are not always the best person for the job. Two classic cases of the wrong man for the job come to mind:

- Tony Haywood, former CEO of BP, whose biggest faux-pas was, despite the injuries, fatalities and lost livelihoods caused by the 2010 Deepwater Horizon Gulf of Mexico BP oil spill, when he said on camera *'I want my life back.* In Hayward's case, just because he was the CEO and running that massive conglomerate, it does not mean that he was necessarily the best person to stand in front of the media as this example shows.
- The second example was by Gary Southern, President of Freedom Industries. His company was responsible for a chemical spillage into the Elk River at Charleston that contaminated drinking water for around 300,000 West Virginia inhabitants. He was clearly trying to avoid answering questions from television reporters explaining

that he had a long day while completely overlooking that many people had had a long day too and without water thanks to his company.

Both of these classic on-screen gaffes have been saved for posterity on YouTube and are a useful source of material for 'how not to do it' training.

Your roles and responsibilities will also need to ensure that however and whoever you are communicating with, your messages are consistent regardless of which communication channels you are using. So do not fall into the trap of saying one thing to TV, radio or press reporters and then contradict yourself via social media.

So let's consider the 'Who'.

The first thing to decide is who exactly are the stakeholders that you will need to communicate with? Your target audiences are likely to be split into internal and external groups such as:

- Staff
- Emergency contacts
- Customers
- Suppliers
- Public
- Press, television, radio

- Shareholders
- Authorities
- Insurers
- Financiers
- Social Media

You will need to record names, their relationship with the organisation, ideally with multiple contact details and their preferred means of receiving information from you especially in a crisis. Some organisations will ask these stakeholders for landline telephone numbers, cell phones, email, Twitter ID etc.

etc. and then promptly use that extra contact information as additional channels for marketing purposes. This may seem unethical and perhaps even far-fetched but I know this happens as it happened to me.

There is also a need to be mindful that in some countries there may be data protection legislation that means it is essential to obtain the contact's explicit permission to include their personal details on a list of this nature. You should also be prepared to offer a clear explanation of how you intend to use this information. Don't forget your staff too. If the crisis you may be called upon to deal with has been an incident that caused injuries and even fatalities amongst your staff, you will also need contact details for next of kin too. Generally speaking, most organisations would expect the responsibility of contacting next of their kin to be picked up by their Human Resources Management teams.

Hopefully there aren't any surprises in the stakeholders list and of course there may well be others that are relevant to your organisations that should be added.

How are we going to communicate?

Define your communication channels and decide on the most appropriate for each stakeholder group, such as:

- Corporate website
- Social media which can be sub-divided into portals such as:
  - Blogs
  - Facebook
  - Twitter
  - YouTube

- Radio
- Television
- Local / National Newspapers
- Trade Journals
- Telephone
- Email

Give some thought to the timings and frequency of communications which may vary across the stakeholder groups. Remember you need to be clear within your organisation about who is responsible for communicating with each stakeholder group and which channel or channels they will be using.

Remember, as an alternative, some organisations actually choose to utilise the services of specialist organisations such as public relations companies to undertake their crisis communications. Your decision on whether to engage a third party could be influenced by the anticipated frequency of crises within your organisation. If it is very low it may pay to outsource your crisis management communications rather than have a team permanently on standby for crises that rarely happen.

Finally, let's move onto the 'What'.

To begin with, define the process that you will need to create and issue media statements. Remember that the crisis may or may not have been caused by social media. In the case of the latter, it may be appropriate to open with a statement especially if the information you are imparting is not yet in the public domain.

If an incident has occurred but it is unclear to your crisis management team exactly what has happened, don't ignore the situation and say nothing at all, don't be indecisive and use expressions like 'we think that' and 'maybe this is because' etc. If you don't know what has happened then say so. Consider the case of Southwest Flight 345 from Nashville to New York La Guardia on 22 July 2013. The plane crash landed on the runway because the nose landing gear touched down and then collapsed before the main landing gear had touched down.

Back at Southwest headquarters, while aware that an incident had occurred involving one of their aircraft, initially no one knew any of the details including whether there had been any injuries or fatalities. So the following tweet was posted:

Figure 7: Southwest Airlines - standby for more information
Source: Twitter

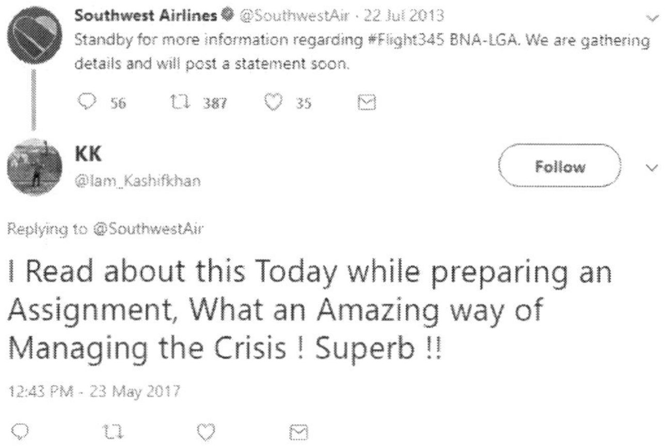

Southwest Airlines ✔ @SouthwestAir · 22 Jul 2013
Standby for more information regarding #Flight345 BNA-LGA. We are gathering
details and will post a statement soon.

♡ 56   ⟲ 387   ♡ 35   ✉

KK   (Follow)   ⌄
@Iam_Kashifkhan

Replying to @SouthwestAir

I Read about this Today while preparing an
Assignment, What an Amazing way of
Managing the Crisis ! Superb !!

12:43 PM · 23 May 2017

♡   ⟲   ♡   ✉

Figure 8: One of many positive responding tweets
Source: Twitter

As Figure 7 shows, Southwest took the initiative and immediately placed themselves on the front foot even though they were not entirely sure about the details of the event. Figure 8 is one of the many positive responses that were posted expressing appreciation in the way in which Southwest airlines was dealing with the incident via Twitter.

Social media guru Jay Baer identifies the first step to take in dealing with a crisis is to issue an **acknowledgement** which Southwest Airlines did even though that had very little detail available that they could post at that time. It is also important to respond in via the channel where the crisis first broke (e.g. Twitter, Facebook etc.) and then follow up on other channels as appropriate. Baer also recommends the creation of a 'Crisis FAQ' on a Web page or microsite and **put all the information**

about the crisis in one place. This allows you to respond to questions with a link instead of an answer. This saves times and prevents misinterpretation of your responses (especially on Twitter). The FAQ should include:

- Acknowledgement of the crisis
- Details about the occurrence
- Photos or videos, if available
- How the company found out
- Who was alerted, when, and how
- Specific actions taken in response
- Real or potential effects
- Steps taken to prevent future occurrence
- Contact information for real people at the company

Source: (Baer, 2012)

There are occasions when people with some form of grievance would prefer to talk to a 'real person' so be prepared to take the dialogue offline and offer them a contact number to call.

Finally, when the crisis is over and the dust has settled, it is time to learn from your experience. You should be looking to identify what went well, what could you perhaps have done better and what went badly. If you find fault with your processes then fix them. Last but by no means least; don't miss an opportunity to extract material from the crisis that you can put to good use in future training exercises.

3.2.4 Tips on Engagement

- **Criticism**: - Receiving criticism via social media must be accepted as a given although how you respond is fundamental and can make a substantial difference to the final outcome. It is important that you should take the criticism in your stride and work to find an answer. It is a positive thing that people care enough to enter into a discussion! Always respond as quickly as possible and courteously point out any erroneous information that has been posted. Also:

- o Explain how you are going to address the criticism
- o Invite further feedback.
- o Don't ignore it or delete the post
- o Don't yell or preach.

- **Handling mistakes**: - Accept the fact that you will make mistakes but don't let this fear stop you – we are only human, and the audience knows that. Section 4.15 provides some examples of human error that resulted in nothing worse than some egg-on-face for the perpetrators. Be prepared to admit that 'we got it wrong' and be swift in making any necessary changes. Learn from the experience!
- **Building credibility:** - Make sure you set up your profile fully, using familiar corporate images and logos. Be transparent – say who you are and who you work for. Add value by sharing tips and insights. Be as accurate as possible
- **Personal Approach:** Use a personal approach. Learn from observing how others speak and interact. Use some pre-prepared responses until you feel comfortable. Think customer not corporate. Inject some fun into your posts where appropriate. Be appreciative of peoples' suggestions and feedback.

On a day-to-day basis providing accurate postings will help to build your credibility with the audience. However, during an emergency people actively look to social media for information that will help them build situation awareness and make decisions. Provide a steady stream of information to them, acknowledging where you are still waiting for facts and confirmations, and then provide updates when you receive them.

Source: (Gov UK, 2012)

3.2.5 When is your crisis management desk open?

There are case studies in sections 4.1 and 4.5 where the organisations concerned ran 24 / 7 commercial aviation operations but it seems their crisis management teams were only geared up to work a 9-to-5 type of shift. As a consequence when both suffered high profile incidents outside of their normal office hours, the world was asking questions and demanding information but nobody was answering. As you can imagine, this reflected badly on both organisations and in one case the absence of communications seem to become more of an issue than the original incident itself in which three people had died and many had been injured.

Please keep in mind that in this so called age of information, people have developed an almost insatiable appetite and expectation for instant responses to their social media complaints and queries. Remember that if you do run some kind of continuous global operation, some of your customers will always be awake which begs the question – can your crisis management team afford to sleep?

4 The best of friends or worst of enemies?

Since crisis management and social media began to collaborate, what has become clear is that social media certainly does not offer itself up as a communications silver bullet. Far from it! While there is no question that social media can be an extremely useful extra communication channel, if it is not effectively managed, it can become an organisation's worst nightmare. Moreover, if an organisation does not have a crisis management communication plan then using social media in the event of a serious incident is probably going to be as useful as a chocolate teapot.

In this chapter a number of case studies have been included that are intended to illustrate the best and the worst of social media that has been experienced in relation to crisis management.

4.1 United screw-up in full view of the world

Twice within the space of two weeks, United Airlines faced two social media firestorms both being of its own making. March, 27th 2017 witnessed what became known as the 'Leggings Gate' incident when two young ladies were barred from boarding a United Airlines flight as they were wearing stretchy leggings. This generated a wave of high profile criticism along with threats to boycott the airline and as one passenger tweeted: "Since when does United police women's clothing?" However, this incident was to diminish into comparative insignificance 13 days later.

If ever an organisation shot itself in the foot while caught in the full glare social media's spotlight, it had to be United Airlines in

2017. On Sunday 9th April Dr David Dao was physically dragged off Flight 3411 from Chicago to Louisville, Kentucky. A number of passengers videoed the incident and long before the aircraft had completed the 285 mile journey (460 km) the story had already gone viral.

> *"This is a terrible situation for any organization to find itself in, but to make matters worse, United showed no semblance of compassion or remorse for their abused customer and, as a result, the Internet is going crazy against the airline and United's Chinese market is cutting up their United Mileage cards in anger"* - *(Agnes, 2017)*

International crisis management strategist Melissa Agnes (2017) maintains that to go viral, a story needs three main components:

- It is emotionally compelling
- It is relatable
- There is a catchy headline, a newsworthy image or a snappy sensitive video

I have long since lost count of the number of commercial flights I have taken – certainly hundreds, possibly even thousands. There have been occasions in my life when it seemed as if I was spending more time in the air than on the ground. Despite all that travelling, I have only ever been bumped off flights on four occasions and by four different airlines – in Amsterdam - KLM, Cologne (Köln) - British Airways, Palermo - Alitalia and Southampton – British Regional Airlines. On another occasion I volunteered to be bumped off as I was quite happy to be paid to extend my holiday on the island of Malta by 24 hours (Air Malta). These personal experiences had occurred before online check-in was universally available and each time, I had been one of the last to check-in and I had been presented with a *'fait accompli'* – "sorry sir, the flight is full" (note to self – check-in early). While it may not have been convenient, I always felt that each of the airlines were very professional in the way they dealt with the situation including appropriate financial compensation, in some instances even before European Union regulations dictated (EU 261, 2004). On two occasions I was subsequently upgraded on the next available flight. But then there was never any chance that I would be physically dragged off any of the aircraft as I never actually boarded.

While airlines have long since been notorious for overbooking flights to compensate for those 'no-show' passengers, every so often, this policy backfires when everyone actually turns up. So just how did United manage to turn what should have been just a routine overbooking scenario into a major crisis? Let's be clear, although their personnel were not physically involved in removing passengers from the aircraft, United essentially caused this crisis themselves because they wanted to free up seats for four of their own employees. With respect to Dr Dao, United performed what it calls an "involuntary denial of the boarding process." Legally, if a flight is overbooked, a passenger can quite legitimately be denied access to the aircraft up to and including the gate. But this is where it gets confusing. The passengers including Dr Dao had already boarded, they were sat in their designated seats and were ready to fly. So how do you deny a passenger from boarding after boarding has already been completed?

It certainly seems that United Airlines had not even got close to occupying either the moral or the legal high ground in this instance. Far from it – although he may not have realised it at the time, as it transpired Dr Dao was holding all the aces!

As it always seems these days, social media was on hand and ready to proliferate the story of United's treatment of Dr Dao across the globe aided and abetted by the numerous videos captured by other passengers. It originally appeared to have been police who forcibly removed the passenger but it later transpired that they were aviation security officers. A Chicago Aviation department spokesman later admitted that standard operating procedures had not been followed and the actions of the security officers were certainly not condoned by the Department (Calfas, 2017). Although it is not clear how many security officers were involved in the incident, it is known that three were subsequently suspended and two were later fired (Spielman, 2017).

> *"As a result of his rough treatment, Dr Dao was hospitalised; and thanks to the multiple smartphone videos that captured the confrontation between Dr Dao and the security officials, the incident has escalated into a global PR disaster for United Airlines"* - *(Delaney, 2017).*

United Airlines took 18 hours to make a statement. Initially it tweeted that "Flight 3411 from Chicago to Louisville was overbooked. After our team looked for volunteers, one customer refused to leave the aircraft voluntarily and law enforcement was asked to come to the gate". This was later followed by an apology for the overbooking situation. Had anyone wanted further details on the 'removed customer' (as United initially referred to Dr Dao) those inquiries should be directed to the authorities (Bradley, 2017).

In all these statements there was no attempt at showing any compassion and, unlike Chicago Aviation Department, nor did the airline initially make any attempt to disassociate itself from the abominable treatment that Dr Dao received.

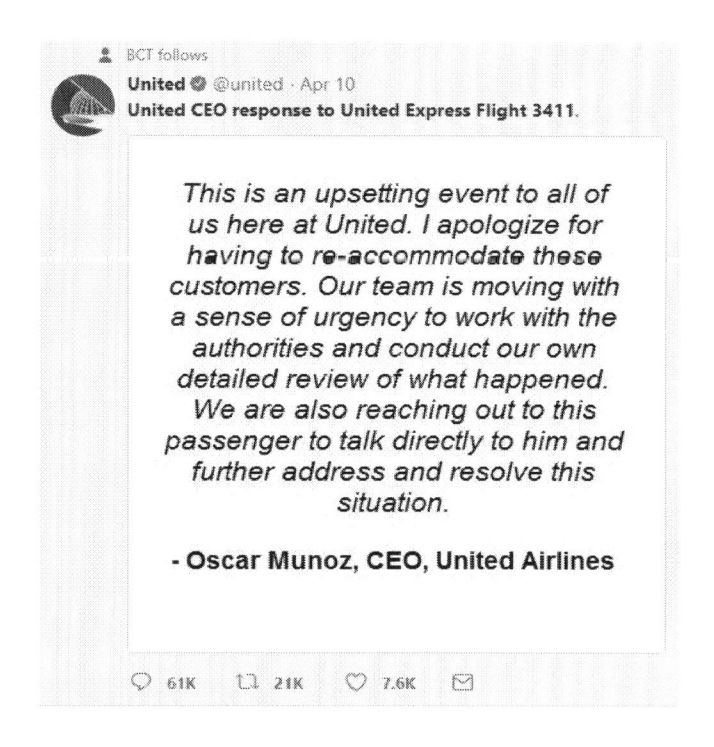

Figure 9: United CEO Twitter response to United Flight 3411
Source: (Twitter, 2017)

It is not clear when exactly United Airlines' crisis management team first became aware of the developing catastrophe. The flight crew on-board 3411 should have flagged up the incident. However, it may have been the dramatic increase in the volume of negative United Airlines targeted social media traffic – assuming that this was being monitored by the company. Clearly, United found itself very rapidly on the back foot which would imply that it was totally unprepared to deal with a crisis of this magnitude. As there was no response from the airline until the following day, it is entirely possible that it was not operating a 24/7 social media presence. Moreover, it never owned or controlled the social media conversation about the incident which is hardly an enviable position for an organisation to be in.

So with the benefit of hindsight, there are a number of valuable lessons that we can we learn from the flight 3411 debacle. For example:

- Any organisation can find itself having to deal with a nasty crisis which may or may not be of its own making. Own up to your mistakes and don't try and pass the buck.
- If your procedures are wrong, admit it and fix them.
- Your crisis management team must be trained and empowered to respond immediately including via social media. You should not be delaying 18 hours before your first response – whatever the cause of the incident may be.
- Think through as many potential scenarios as is practical and draft announcements, Twitter feeds and Facebook statements etc. and enable your Crisis Management team to practice and practice and then practice again.

- Large airlines are likely to have aircraft in the air somewhere in the world at all times of the day and night. If you are running a global 24/7 operation you need a crisis management team including social media specialists available to respond to incidents as they occur, wherever and whenever they occur. There is no point having a 24/7 operation if you only have something resembling a 9-to-5 crisis management and social media response capability.

- For an airline possibly a worst case scenario would be one of its aircraft crashing and resulting in serious injuries and fatalities. This is especially true when its social media capability is offline as the demand for information and pressure on the organisation will spiral (please refer to section 4.5). But there are naturally other crises that do not involve aircraft crashing but which can still put an organisation in a bad light. Flight 3411 is a point in case of course. Either way, you need to be ready to deal with situations quickly, effectively and compassionately. If you are unsure what exactly has happened, be prepared to issue a 'holding statement' while you investigate and find out what has been going on. The worst possible thing is to do is to say nothing as to some that may imply you are doing nothing. When you finally make a statement, be honest and do not bullshit as you will invariably be found out.

- At least United appear to have come to a settlement with Dr Dao and their gesture of refunding all other passengers will do them no harm either. However, they may still get sued.

The longer you take to respond in a crisis, the bigger the crisis is likely to become and potentially the more expensive to fix. But all this could have been avoided. Had United chartered an aircraft to fly their employees from Chicago to Louisville rather than bump the four passengers, yes there would have been a cost involved, but it would have preserved the company's reputation and saved probably many millions of dollars into the bargain.

It is usually worth trying to make a point of learning from your competitors' misfortunes and United's competitors certainly didn't miss a trick vis-à-vis flight 3411. Within days, American Airlines announced that passengers who have boarded will not be removed to allow someone else to take their seat. Delta announced that gate agents have been authorized to pay up to $2,000 to entice passengers to relinquish seats on overbooked flights. In some situations, with appropriate supervisory approval, that limit can be raised to nearly $10,000 - (Perkins, 2017). Generous incentives like this this might even encourage some people to try and make a career out of being bumped off aircraft.

After the story had broken, United Airlines' shares plummeted when the markets opened the following day wiping around $1 Billion off the company's value. But they quickly rallied and were only 4% down when trading closed. Moreover, while two days before the incident on Friday 7th April 2017 shares had been valued at $67.40, two months later on 7th June they were trading at $81.66 (Source: NYSE). Certainly the behaviour of the stock markets suggest that it seemed indifferent to the flight

3411 incident indicating that United will invariably survive this debacle.

While Dr Dao received an undisclosed out of court settlement which, given the circumstances, one hopes was substantial, all other passengers on 3411 were refunded the cost of their flight. That said, unless United has persuaded these passengers to sign a waiver as a condition of the refund, it would not surprise me if claims were later pursued for trauma brought on by being subjected to the despicable handling of the situation.

But what will the real cost have been to the company? Primarily one would have expected it will have been a combination of damaged reputation and lost revenue largely from reduced bookings due to the outrage it caused across the world. Yet three months later the New York Times reporter James Stewart observed:

"Within days, the Twitter hashtag #BoycottUnited had been used over 3.5 million times…..So when United reported second quarter earnings last week, many investors feared results might go off a cliff just as the peak travel season was getting underway. But they were surprisingly robust. Revenue rose over 6 percent and profits shot up 49%. There are no signs of any boycott. The airline said it had 71 million passengers in the first half of the year, 4.2 percent more than the previous year" - (Stewart, 2017)

In the longer term, we humans are often guilty of having very short and perhaps even selective memories. Immediately after the 2004 Indian Ocean tsunami killed around 250,000 the tourist beaches in the area were empty. But before long those missing tourists went back – many lured initially by cheap deals. Tourism also died in Israel in the year 2000 during the second intifada (Arab uprising) but as soon as it was over, once again the tourists went back. So what of the many thousands around the world who were outraged by seeing the flight 3411 incident played out on social media? I am sure that many will have vowed that United Airlines would never get any business from them. But time will pass and with it those memories of Dr Dao being dragged off the aircraft will fade. So perhaps the next time they are planning a trip somewhere and United just happen to be offering the best deal in town, just maybe the resilience of their principals will not stand the passage of time. In fact judging by Stewart's observation in the New York Times, United seems to be financially better off for the experience.

Perhaps if American and Delta airlines had waited to see the longer term effect of the two United Airlines faux-pas, they may not have been in such a rush to generously increase their 'denial of boarding' compensation offerings. The old adage tells us that "there is no such thing as bad publicity" although sometimes I find that difficult to believe. But with its share price up, passenger numbers up and revenue up, despite all the negative media coverage, just maybe United Airlines has succeeded in epitomising that adage.

4.2 Virgin Trains strike the right balance

On a day-to-day basis, organisations like Virgin Trains use a one-to-one approach to communicate with their customers on Twitter. When a crisis occurs, if the situation demands, they can switch to a broadcast style to avoid being swamped by an increase in Twitter traffic.

On Monday 18th December 2017, I was travelling from Manchester Piccadilly to London Euston on Virgin Trains – a journey that normally takes around 2 hours. The train made an unscheduled stop at Milton Keynes and passengers were informed by the on-board staff that there had been an incident on the railway at Hemel Hempstead station where someone had been hit by a train. The emergency services were at the scene and all train services on the line into London Euston had been suspended until further notice. We later learned that the individual struck by the train had been declared dead at the scene and British Transport Police were not treating the incident as suspicious.

This was the second occasions that I had experienced delays on this route as the result of a fatality and while the deaths are regrettable, I must say that I have been impressed with Virgin Trains' management of the crises. Figure 10 shows the Tweet that Virgin issued immediately the story broke on December 18, 2017. Reciprocal agreements already exist between Virgin and other rail companies and when appropriate they will invariably be activated when some form of disruption occurs. After the line was reopened, my train ultimately arrived at London Euston around two hours late.

When I previously experienced a similar delay my train bound from London to Manchester was yet to depart from Euston station. In addition to social media broadcasts, announcements were made on-board and via the station PA system keeping travellers informed. I ultimately arrived in Manchester having switched to another train company and travelled from London's Kings Cross station via Leeds.

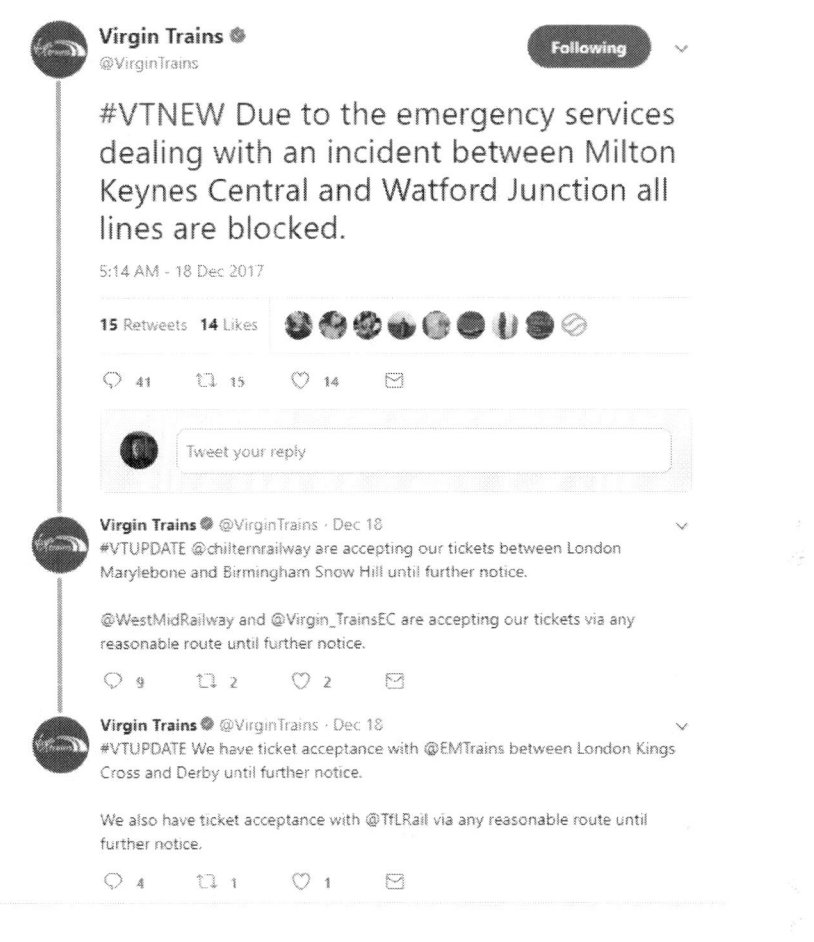

Figure 10: @VirginTrains tweet re: incident at Hemel Hempstead
Source: (Twitter, 2017)

4.3 Al Shabaab live-tweet terrorist attack

On Saturday 21st September 2013, a very undesirable and dark side of social media's multi-faceted capability became apparent. Using Twitter, the al Qaeda affiliated al Shabaab terrorist group live-tweeted a running commentary of its attack on the Westgate shopping mall in Nairobi, Kenya. Consequently the story of the massacre hit the social media platform before being picked up by the more traditional media channels. Using guns and grenades the terrorist killed more than sixty people and injured close to two-hundred in a siege that lasted for four days.

Al-Shabaab is acknowledged as being very savvy in the use of social media and had clearly planned ahead. When the attack started it was tweeting on @HSMPress (the HSM stands for "*Harakat al-Shabaab al-Mujahideen*"). By the following morning Twitter had closed down the account only for the terrorists to almost immediately reappear having switched to @HSM_PressOffice.

> *"The* Somalia-*based organisation provided an extraordinary running commentary of the attacks on Twitter – glorifying the militants, taunting the Kenyan security forces, and justifying their actions" - (Alexander, 2013)*

Ordinary Kenyan citizens had learned how to use social media and other digital tools to amplify their voices in order to have impact within the country. They frequently go on line to share information. For example, they had previously used Twitter to organize carpooling during a strike by public transport operators and even to find out which petrol stations had stocks of fuel during fuel shortages (Were, 2013).

In fact, research by Portland and Tweetminster two year earlier had revealed that within Africa, Kenya's use of Twitter was second only to South Africa. Inside the mall, trapped shoppers turned to social media for help and many were texting their positions to authorities hoping for rescue. Consequently, the local population would have been only too well aware of what was happening at Westgate.

> *"Those in the mall and its environs flooded their Twitter, Facebook and Instagram accounts with text and images"* - (Were, 2013)

So should we consider that this use of live-tweeting by al-Shabaab was a one off? Personally, I believe that if it suits their mode of attack, other terrorist groups may also be tempted to adopt a similar approach to maximise the publicity their actions receive. While each terrorist group will have overarching objectives which may or may not be politically, religiously or nationalistically motivated, Savitch suggests that most individual terrorist strikes will invariably look to achieve three goals. He refers to these as:

- Catalytic terrorism – in full view of the media
- Mega terrorism – maximise human casualties
- Smart Terrorism – maximise critical asset damage

Source: (Savitch, 2008)

The history of terrorism can point to some exceptions to Savitch's three goal model. For example, evaluation of the Irish Republican Army's 1990's UK Mainland bombing campaign demonstrates that the targets were primarily economic. The campaign did not aim to achieve a Mega Terrorism goal as coded warnings minimised human casualties. With an estimated seventy five thousand evacuated from the City Centre before the bomb exploded, without prior warning, the potential casualties from the 1996 Manchester bombing in the UK could have been horrific (BBC - On This Day, 2008).

There is no doubt that the Westgate Shopping Mall attack achieved all three of Savitch's goals. Moreover, al Shabaab's social media strategy not only maximised their efforts in achieving the 'catalytic' goal, they also ensured that they not only owned the story but they forced Kenyan authorities onto the back foot.

> **Author's Note**:
>
> The Economic and Social Research Council (ESRC) has observed that social media is becoming a key information source for the public when violent terror acts occur. At its peak, there were in excess of 800 tweets a minute about the murder by terrorists of British Army soldier Lee Rigby in London in 2013 (ESRC, 2015).

4.4 Can Social Media Cause a PR Crisis

"Studies show that almost 40% of crisis in 16 countries including the United States and China result from either negative publicity on social media or digital security failures" - (Cheng & Cameron, 2017)

While every social media *'mistake'* tends to be unique, Digital Eye has identified a few common denominators that are characteristic of a Public Relations disaster just waiting to happen. For example:

i. Inappropriate or insensitive posts or tweets about sensitive or inflammatory topics that inspire strong emotions from the audience.
ii. Unintended consequences or reactions generated from seemingly harmless post content.
iii. Unintentional posting of personal content to business social media accounts.

Source: (Digital EYE, 2015)

4.4.1 Inflammatory personal view tweeted on company's Twitter account

One example of social media creating a public relations crisis actually combines points i) and iii) in section 4.14.3. It involved KitchenAid, an American home appliance brand owned by Whirlpool Corporation. The company found itself acutely embarrassed by a very insensitive joke tweeted by one of its employees using the company's Twitter account. During a debate in the US 2012 Presidential election campaign, President Obama had mentioned his grandmother, Madelyn Lee Payne Dunham who had raised him from when he was aged 10. Apparently she had sadly died November 2nd 2008, just before Obama was elected president.

There follows the original offensive tweet followed by the text of the two official tweets and a Facebook apology released by KitchenAid. We are also led to believe that errant Tweet resulted from the employee mistakenly using the company Twitter account rather than their own.

KitchenAid
@KitchenAidUSA

Obamas gma even knew it was going 2 b bad! 'She died 3 days b4 he became president'. #nbcpolitics

Figure 11: Offensive tweet about Barack Obama's grandmother
Source: Twitter

KitchenAid reacted quickly and issued the tweet : "Deepest apologies for an irresponsible tweet that is in no way a representation of the brand's opinion. #nbcpolitics".

A second tweet followed shortly afterwards: "I would like to personally apologies to President @BarackObama, his family and everyone on Twitter for the offensive tweet sent earlier."

Finally the Facebook entry reinforced the apology in the second official tweet (see Figure 12). It was shared 130 times, received 969 likes and generated almost two thousand comments which, although some were expressing understanding and support, not all were positive responses.

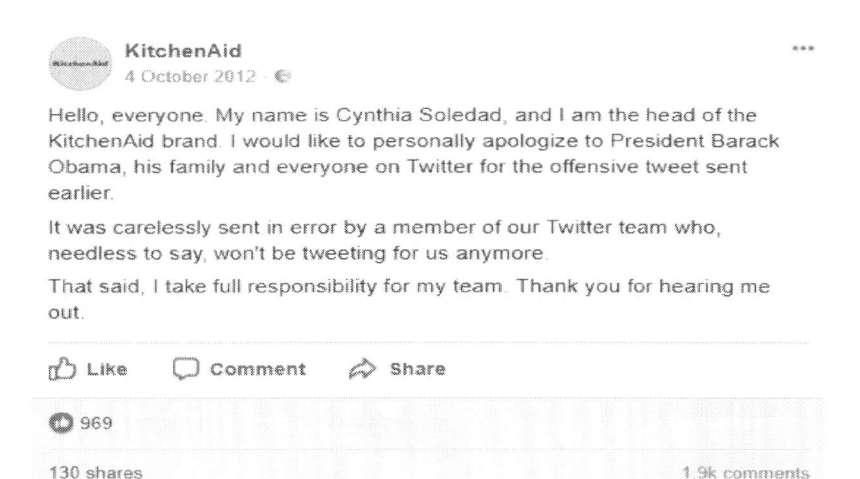

KitchenAid
4 October 2012

Hello, everyone. My name is Cynthia Soledad, and I am the head of the KitchenAid brand. I would like to personally apologize to President Barack Obama, his family and everyone on Twitter for the offensive tweet sent earlier.

It was carelessly sent in error by a member of our Twitter team who, needless to say, won't be tweeting for us anymore.

That said, I take full responsibility for my team. Thank you for hearing me out.

Like   Comment   Share

969

130 shares   1.9k comments

Figure 12: Facebook apology issued by KitchenAid
Source: Facebook

> *"By being swift, candid and up-front, they were able to minimize the impact of the initial tweet, show their genuine concern and prevent any lasting damage to the brand" – Ray Holmes, CEO at Hootsuite.*

4.4.2   Getting a bad TripAdvisor review scares me

I am a regular visitor to the island of Malta and recently I was travelling to the airport and used a new taxi service that had been recommended by a friend. The driver and taxi owner was a one man band and somehow we got talking about social media. Quite understandably, building and maintaining his reputation for delivering a good service was important to him. But he lived in fear of what might be posted on social media about him and his taxi service to the extent that he admitted it often caused some sleepless nights.

I think we need to accept that we cannot please everyone all the time. Even if our services and products are first rate, once in a while getting a negative review should be looked upon as an occupational hazard. But the taxi man has a point insofar as too many negative reviews could ruin his business which for him would be a crisis. In fact,

> *"TripAdvisor can make or break a business if you have too many bad reviews people aren't going to be interested in attending your establishment"* - *(Beech, 2018)*

I told him that if I am looking to go somewhere or use a service that is unfamiliar to me, perhaps a restaurant or a hotel, I invariably use TripAdvisor to see what experiences other people have had. If the reviews weigh heavily on the positive side then I am less inclined to take the negative seriously. A favourite restaurant of mine in Malta has received awards from TripAdvisor for its excellence. But once in a while it gets a disappointing review but that has never stopped me from continuing my patronage. Bad reviews can happen – get over it!

At the other end of the scale, one UK hotel in Blackpool, the Broadway Hotel, caused a stir by charging guests £100 sterling for leaving a bad review. One couple, Tony and Jan Jenkinson, called it a *"rotten stinking hovel"* and listed a catalogue of things they found wrong with their room only to later find that the hotel had added the £100 charge to their credit card (Quinn, 2014). As of 1st January 2018, fifty-nine percent of the hotel's TripAdvisor reviews had been terrible. The comments posted included *"the hotel from hell"*, *"never again"*, *"absolutely disgusting"* and *"should be closed down"* (TripAdvisor, 2018).

4.4.3 The tale of two banks

September 2007 saw the first run on a UK bank for 150 years. Northern Rock had requested and had received a liquidity support facility from the Bank of England which was designed to compensate for funds that the bank had been unable to raise on the open money market. The news of the bank's request leaked out leading to panic among its depositors. Fearing the bank might collapse, many believed that their funds would be lost should Northern Rock go into receivership.

There were many who pointed the finger at the BBC's former business editor, Robert Peston, for causing the run on the bank. At the time of the Northern Rock incident, Peston not only had a prominent and influential position with the BBC, but he also had a substantial social media following which numbered in the hundreds of thousands.

> *"The British Bankers' Association has singled out Mr Peston and the BBC for acting 'injudiciously' in reporting the problems at Northern Rock"* - (BBC News, 2009)

Peston argued that Northern Rock would likely have collapsed irrespective of whether there had been that run. However, despite all the finger pointing in his direction, it seems to me that all he was guilty of was breaking the Northern Rock story which also happened to be a news scoop. Unless, UK national security had been threatened (which it wasn't) there was no reason why Peston should not have broken the story which most other journalist given the chance would have done too. Moreover, he did not cause the problems that forced Northern Rock to approach the Bank of England in the first instance.

But I feel that this is worthy of comparison with an incident concerning the Bank of Albuquerque (BoA) that occurred in February 2014. On his programme for Next News Network (N[3]), broadcaster Gary Franchi talked about an email received from the BoA by a friend. Via the email, the BoA was advising its customers that it was planning to conduct a 'disaster preparedness drill' over the weekend of 15th / 16th February 2014. Showing his complete lack of in-depth knowledge about the subject, Franchi tells his audience that "banks don't normally do disaster preparedness drills" and there may well have been an alternative and perhaps even sinister agenda in action. Clearly, he was unaware that banks have to run business continuity, disaster recovery and emergency preparedness exercises because they have no choice as they are regulated. Even so, he erroneously goes onto to explain that in the USA only organisations such as FEMA, State Agencies or Federal Agencies conduct these emergency disaster preparedness exercises. He concludes his 3 minute sound bite by suggesting that people take their money out the bank!

	FRANCHI	N³	PESTON	BBC
Twitter followers	4 K	10 K	900 K	22 million
Target Bank	Bank of Albuquerque		Northern Rock	
Perceived damage	None		Blamed for causing run on the bank	

Figure 13: Peston and Franchi comparison of traditional and social media influence (2015)

I must admit that I have found it nigh on impossible to quantify and provide a meaningful comparison of the audience sizes of N³ and the BBC especially with the global reach of the latter. Nor was it possible to retrospectively establish the actual size of the respective Twitter followings in 2007 and 2014. Consequently the figures quoted in Figure 13 were as of 1st January 2018. However, a straight forward numerical comparison of the Twitter following between Robert Peston and Gary Franchi as individuals plus the organisational clout of the BBC versus Next News Network shows a massive disparity in social media reach alone. Consequently I believe it is safe to assume that the size of audience that the two stories would have reached were very disproportionate. With his impressive Twitter following, arguably Robert Peston could have triggered the bank run even without the support of the BBC behind him.

While Robert Peston's exposé was reporting on a story which had been verified, Gary Franchi's news was based upon a flawed understanding of the subject and was leaning strongly towards the sensational. For all intents and purposes, it was bordering on fake news which is covered in more details in section 4.12.

4.5 Don't Let Communications Become the Crisis

David Eun @Eunner · 6 Jul 2013

I just crash landed at SFO. Tail ripped off. Most everyone seems fine. I'm ok. Surreal... (at @flySFO) [pic] —

Path photo by David

I just crash landed at SFO. Tail ripped off. Most everyone seems fine. I'm ok. Surreal... - at San Francisco International Airport (SFO) (San Francisco

path.com

♡ 2.6K   ↑↓ 30K   ♡ 4.0K   ✉

Figure 14: Tweet by passenger escaping from crashed aircraft
Source: Twitter

This study is an extract from an example that I included in my book entitled *Validating Your Business Continuity Plan*. I feel that it is a very good illustration of an organisation allowing its crisis communications, or in this case, 'the lack of' crisis communications, to almost become bigger than the story itself.

In the case of Asiana Flight OZ 214 flight from Seoul, South Korea, crashing at San Francisco International Airport, 6 July 2013, the first report and photograph appeared on Twitter a full two minutes before the emergency evacuation slides had been deployed by cabin crew. The aircraft was a Boeing 777-200ER, registration HL7742, and was carrying 16 crew and 291 passengers.

When a crisis strikes, the speed at which social media can be exploited to 'spread the news' can be breath-taking. The subsequent tweet by one of the surviving passengers, David Eun @Eunner (see Figure 14), was retweeted over 30,000 times, received over 2,600 comments and was quickly picked up by several major television news networks, such as the BBC, CNN, Sky News and NBC.

The National Transportation Safety Board issued statements on social media within one hour of the crash. Aircraft manufacturer Boeing and the local fire department also promptly made statements via social media. But nothing was heard from the airline.

Such was the intensity of related information searches, the airline, Asiana, was almost instantly put on the back foot. A similar experience happened at Glasgow Airport in the UK after the 2007 attempted bombing. The traffic to the airport website alone rose from an average of 6,000 hits per week to 130,000 during the week immediately following the incident.

The crash occurred around 11:20 am San Francisco local time so with Seoul in South Korea 17 hour ahead, it was 04:20 am at Asiana's Headquarters. However, it was after 08:00 am Seoul time, four hours after the incident, before Asiana broke its silence when it posted a comment on Facebook. A further five hours later the airline issued a press statement.

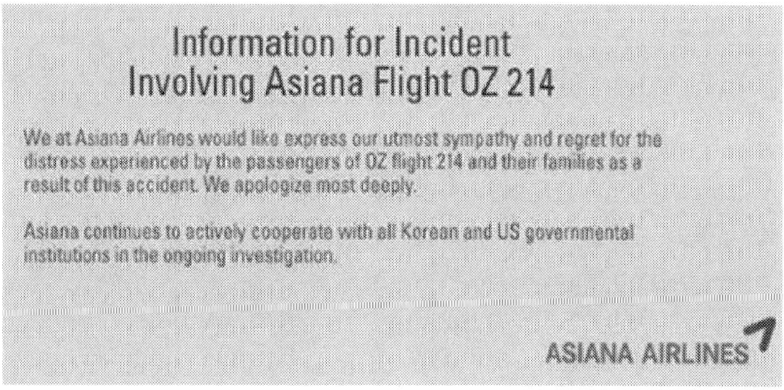

**Information for Incident
Involving Asiana Flight OZ 214**

We at Asiana Airlines would like express our utmost sympathy and regret for the distress experienced by the passengers of OZ flight 214 and their families as a result of this accident. We apologize most deeply.

Asiana continues to actively cooperate with all Korean and US governmental institutions in the ongoing investigation.

ASIANA AIRLINES

Figure 15: Asiana Airlines Facebook post
Source: Facebook

"Tell it all, tell it fast and tell the truth." (Hicks, 2006)

With three fatalities and 49 serious injuries, what can be learned from this catastrophic situation? First and foremost, it would seem that despite running a 24/7 global airline operation, Asiana's crisis management capability did not match this round the clock service. So it appears that until the normal business day started in Korea, Asiana was not in a position to respond.

In this age of virtually instant news reporting, the speed of communication is essential. There is a growing expectation that your organisation will respond instantaneously with all the facts and report them honestly. Failure to do so may be interpreted, although possibly unjustly, in a number of negative ways, such as you are unprepared, not in control of the situation, or that you have adopted an overly casual and indifferent attitude.

It must be remembered that many of your stakeholders will be demanding answers or reassurance. Any delays in information dissemination may be interpreted as reluctance or an inability to act decisively. This in turn could be seen as being symptomatic of a questionable ability, in this case of operating an airline. Moreover, you will need to be actively following the popular social media websites, such as Twitter and Facebook to monitor what disparaging remarks are being made about your organisation, especially by accounts that have large followings.

> *"Fail to communicate effectively and you risk losing the trust and confidence of your customers, or worse: your company's reputation takes a nose dive." (Finegan, 2013)*

4.6 The Insider Threat

In my book *"In Hindsight – a compendium of business continuity case studies"* I recounted the story of a disgruntled market research company employee who went around his employers premises spraying IT equipment with the corrosive cleaner *Cillit Bang*. Over a three year period between 2009 and 2012, the damage he caused was extensive and resulted in considerable expense and inconvenience to his employer. He was finally caught only after CCTV was installed. Even so, unlike a more high profile incident such as an organisation's head office burning down, his malicious attacks went largely unnoticed by the outside world.

Being in the information age, consider what damage that employee could have caused had his weapon of choice been his employers social media platform rather than *Cillit Bang*. While on the one hand he would have most probably been caught a lot sooner, the bad news is that by pumping out a few well worded Tweets or Facebook entries he could have seriously damaged his employer's business.

But it has happened to other organisations as the following examples illustrate. Domino's Pizza is a classic case of employees damaging the company's reputation via social media creating a nightmare experience for the company. Two employees, Kristy Hammonds and Michael Setzer, were employed by Domino's Pizza at Conover, North Carolina. Between them they made and posted a video on YouTube that went viral. It very graphically shows them preparing sandwiches using cheese that had put up his nose, plus coughing and sneezing over the food and Setzer wiping his buttocks with a sponge used for cleaning dishes.

Both Hammonds and Setzer were fired and charged with the distribution of prohibitive foods although they insist that none of the food was ever served to customers. Even so, the health department closed the restaurant to be sanitised.

"Having 21,000 employees around the country that work for us, all of them are doing it the right way and then two idiots make it a really hard day for a lot of us" - Shane Graham, Domino's Franchisee Managing Partner.

Patrick Doyle, President, Domino USA posted a text book response on social media where he apologizes for the incident, and describes the steps his company was taking to ensure such an incident doesn't happen again. He thanked members of the online community for quickly alerting the company about the disgusting video posted by Hammonds and Setzer.

> *"It sickens me that the actions of two individuals could impact our great system. There are so many people who have come through with messages of support for us and we want to thank you for hanging in there as we work to regain your trust" – Patrick Doyle*

Domino's plight is by no means unique. Three teenage female Kentucky Fried Chicken employees posted images on Myspace of them bathing in a KFC sink used for cleaning dishes. They were subsequently fired. Their prank may well have been inspired by an earlier Myspace posting of a male Burger King employee taking a bath in one of the company's industrial sinks. He was also dismissed.

4.7 Hacked twitter account displays rival logo

> *"US fast-food company Burger King has said its Twitter account may have been hacked, after its profile picture was changed to a McDonald's logo" - (BBC News, 2013)*

I feel that the above quote attributed to Burger King by the BBC is something of an understatement. However, person or persons unknown managed to hack Burger King's twitter account and in addition to changing the logo to rival Macdonald's, they tweeted that BK had indeed been sold to its competitor. The hackers then proceeded to Tweet McDonald's special offers along with a flurry of dubious and offensive tweets. A social media consultant from the Wendy's burger chain remarked that his real life nightmare was playing out over on @BurgerKing - (Arthur, 2013).

Meanwhile, McDonald's tweeted in response to the apparent hack: "We empathize with our @BurgerKing counterparts. Rest assured, we had nothing to do with the hacking" - (BBC News, 2013).

The Burger King Twitter account was suspended and the hoax tweets stopped after about an hour and, now five years on, there does not seem to be any lasting damage. However, this should act as a reminder to all organisations that security around their social media accounts, especially password management, is of paramount importance.

Some four years later, McDonald's was claiming that its own Twitter account had been compromised by a hacker. NBC News reported that on 16th March 2017, the following tweet was posted:

 **McDonald's** ✓
@McDonaldsCorp

 👤⁺ Follow ∨

@realDonaldTrump You are actually a disgusting excuse of a President and we would love to have @BarackObama back, also you have tiny hands.

RETWEETS LIKES
21   23

9:16 AM - 16 Mar 2017

↩ 10   🔁 21   ♥ 23

Figure 16: McDonald's anti-Trump hacked tweet
Source: (Zoppo, 2017)

Within an hour McDonald's had deleted the tweet and issued an apology but not before it had been retweeted over 1,000 times (Zoppo, 2017). Apparently not being satisfied with just posting the tweet, the hacker confidently pinned it to top of McDonald's profile, ensuring that everyone on Twitter who wanted to learn about the return of the McRib would see it. Before the tweet was removed it received plenty of 'love' although it also managed to start the hashtag #BoycottMcDonalds by Trump supporters across the country (Shelton, 2017).

4.8 Carry on marketing regardless ?

In 1979, long before the dawn of social media, I was on board an Austrian Airways flight from London Heathrow to Vienna. We had begun our final descent and the cabin crew were busy doing their safety checks – seats upright, arm rests down, seat belts buckled up etc. Without any warning, it felt as though a giant hand had grabbed the aircraft, given it a good shaking and then thrown it up in the air. The experience seemed to last a lifetime although in reality it was probably no more than a few seconds. When I started flying like so many other people I was nervous. But then a friend who was also a British Airways captain suggested to me that if the cabin crew looked happy likely as not everything was alright. Well this suggestion made perfect sense to me and I have used it to good effect ever since. However, on this occasion the cabin crew did not look happy in fact one was catapulted across the row of seats immediately to my right. I recall that one of the passengers she landed on screamed loudly although I'm not sure if it was the shock of the experience or whether she was hurt by the impact. Then just as quickly as it had happened it was all over and we continued our descent and landed without further incident. As we were taxiing to our allocated gate the Captain came over the PA system and apologised for the violent manoeuvre explaining that it had been necessary to avoid a head-on collision. I expect you can imagine that that plane was full of some very scared passengers. Unbelievably, it was at this point that the Senior Stewardess hit us with the standard patter that went something like:

> *"We do hope you have enjoyed your flight and we look forward welcoming you onto an Austrian Airways flight again very soon"*

OK, so the incident probably wasn't the fault of Austrian Airways but I think I can speak for most if not all the other passengers when I say **NO** we had not enjoyed our flight and this certainly was not a very well timed piece of marketing. Yet today social media has made this type of error of judgement so much easier to make. Moreover, it can offend so many more people than the hundred or so that I travelled with on that flight to Vienna.

Thirty-four years later, in 2013 the world was shocked by the news of the Boston Marathon bombing. Many companies closed down their Twitter feeds out of respect although not all and some consequently felt the rage of their followers for being insensitive. Adidas even emailed participants with the message "Congrats, you survived the Boston Marathon!" The following tweet is one of many and very effectively captures the mood:

Figure 17: Typical response to Adidas Boston Marathon email Source: (Oregan Sports, 2017)

Food manufacturer Epicurious was another to be heavily criticised for tweeting messages like "In honour of Boston and New England may we suggest whole-grain cranberry scones!" and "Boston, are hearts are with you.

Here's a bowl of breakfast energy we could all use to start today" – Source: Twitter.

ADWEEK's Elizabeth Mitchell struggled to understand how someone at Epicurious could believe that their suggestion that a recipe for cranberry scones or a bowl of cereal could in some way alleviate the sense of shock, fear and loss that swept Boston. It might have even been laughable if it weren't so terrible. And then, instead of making real, human apologies or taking any meaningful steps to backtrack or make up for their offense, Epicurious chose to simply tweet the same cookie-cutter *"mea culpa"* pleas over and over again. Even this half-hearted apology is bristling – the company apologizes that its tweets "seemed offensive", not that they *were* offensive, as if their outraged followers were overreacting to a harmless message. Unbelievable!

> *"Why, for the love of all that is decent, human, and empathetic, haven't brands figured out that it is never okay to exploit a tragedy that irreversibly altered and ended human lives?" - (Mitchell, 2013)*

Social media coach, consultant and speaker Eric Tung, says companies should pause all scheduled posts in the aftermath of a national or international tragedy:

> *"In these cases, it can seem insensitive, if not downright rude, to continue posting promotional posts when others are in mourning. Even worse, your posts could be seen - whether intended or not - to be playing off the tragedy"* - (Messanger Garrett, 2017).

4.9 Mustard lovers close ranks

In the UK Greater Manchester town of Sale is where you will find Mustard, an American style diner, owned and run by a husband and wife team. On 13th January 2018, a post about Mustard was left on TripAdvisor. Someone using the identifier 'PippaLee77' gave the restaurant a miserable one star rating explaining that her grievance was follows:

> *"Heard good things but website says can't book and just turn up. Wanted to visit for my birthday with family so thought I'd risk it as thought wouldn't be too busy in Jan. got there and it was an hours wait at 5pm! Couldn't wait that long with two hungry children. We went elsewhere in the end which was lovely. I recommend that they introduce a booking system as I won't be visiting again as I wouldn't risk not being able to get a table!"* - (TripAdvisor, 2018).

Strange as it may seem, because the restaurant works on a first come first served basis and was full due to its popularity, PippaLee77 still felt it deserved that miserly rating despite not having actually eaten at Mustard.

The TripAdvisor post was reposted on the restaurant's Facebook page and, in a rather humorous tongue-in-cheek response, Mustard thanked PippaLee77 for what was arguably some great publicity. She had broadcast to the world that, even though it was only 5 pm in the evening (not exactly prime dining time), the restaurant was already packed out with customers.

But things didn't end there. Disgusted Mustard customers responded in their dozens not just to rebuke PippaLee77 for her comments but also to express their support for the restaurant by leaving comments like:

- "*We love Mustard*" - (Laura Madds),
- "*Mustard is a favourite of ours, lovely food and lovely people*" – (Sophie Marion)
- "*I would give you 6 stars. Amazing food, Amazing staff!*" – (Gary Stubbs)
- "*I'd definitely wait an hour for the food! It's delicious!*" – (Emma Crew)

Source: (Facebook, 2018).

So not unlike the United Airlines case study in section 4.1, but for very different reasons, perhaps here is another example of *'there is no such thing as bad publicity'*.

4.10 Who'd be a soccer referee?

"You cannot please all the people all of the time" says the old proverb. Some would argue that professional soccer referees may find it difficult if not impossible to please anyone any of the time. Of course, despite being described as the loneliest job in soccer, without them there would be no soccer. Yet week in week out, these often much maligned individuals are called upon to perform a very difficult job – making split seconds decisions that can often alienate players and supporters alike. But they are human and can make mistakes just like the rest of us. To survive in the game, they have to be prepared to tolerate verbal abuse and sometimes even physical abuse too.

"From the local park to the country's biggest stadiums, referees are shouted at by players, managers and fans alike" – (Marsh, 2017)

One high profile incident occurred in 2004 that involved the very experienced Swedish referee Anders Frisk who was officiating for the Champions League tie between Roma and Dynamo Kiev. As Frisk was walking off the pitch at half time, a coin was thrown from the crowd which struck him on the head. The consequential wound bled heavily and the match was subsequently abandoned. After a separate incident, Frisk announced his decision to quit refereeing the following year after receiving death threats against himself and his family this time from Chelsea fans (Campbell, 2005). This is by no means an isolated case and many other referees from all levels of the sport can recount similar stories of intimidation. In one extreme case, it was also reported that a referee, César Flores, was shot dead by a player he had just sent off in an amateur match in Argentina (Guardian Sport, 2016).

If all this wasn't enough, now social media has entered the fray too. One of the downsides of social media has been the rise of the 'Troll'. This is someone who looks to create conflict on social media platforms such as Twitter and Facebook. Typically they would post messages that are particularly controversial or provocative and not necessarily true, making statements that have the sole intent of provoking an emotional reaction from other users. In many cases they try to hide behind what they consider to be the anonymity of the Internet to target a business or just one person.

Referee Piero Giacomelli infuriated Lazio soccer fans when he showed their forward Ciro Immobile a red card for violent conduct and sent him off just before half time. However, before dismissing Immobile, referee Giacomelli did review the incident with the video assistant referee, before deciding to show the Lazio player a straight red card. To add insult to injury, he then refused to award a penalty to Lazio for a hand ball incident. Lazio went on to lose the match 1-3 to Torino and fans initially took to Twitter to vent their frustrations and anger. Later they switched to TripAdvisor and targeted the café he ran, the Café Rossetti in Trieste, in an attempt to damage the reputation of his business. One Lazio supporter wrote:

"The chef decided to send out a meal which was indecorous and difficult to choke down... Despite the numerous complaints from me and my friends, who were dissatisfied with that incomprehensible dish, the chef decided to send us away in the middle of the evening while still making us pay a large bill" - (BBC News, 2017)

TripAdvisor was quick to respond and suspended the Café Rossetti's profile putting the following message in its place:

Café Rossetti - CHIUSO

<u>Messaggio da TripAdvisor</u>

A causa di un evento recente che ha attirato l'attenzione dei media e causato un afflusso di recensioni che non descrivono un'esperienza in prima persona, abbiamo temporaneamente sospeso la pubblicazione di nuove recensioni per questo profilo. Se hai avuto un'esperienza diretta presso questa struttura e vuoi lasciare un contributo, riprova a breve. Non vediamo l'ora di ricevere la tua recensione

Figure 18: TripAdvisor suspends Café Rossetti's profile
Source: TripAdvisor

The original TripAdvisor message was posted in Italian as illustrated in **Figure 18**. The English translation is as follows:

"Due to a recent event that has attracted media attention and caused an influx of reviews that do not describe a first-hand experience, we have temporarily suspended posting new reviews for this profile. If you have had a direct experience at this structure and you want to leave a contribution, try again soon. We look forward to receiving your review"

The final twist in this tale was that Giacomelli apparently no longer has anything to do with Café Rossetti. But for TripAdvisor's intervention, the current management of the café may have been left shocked and bewildered by all the negative feedback that they were suddenly receiving. Among a number of new one-star reviews were statements like "a nightmare" and "stay far away from this café" (Football Italia Staff, 2017).

4.11 Prison sentences for social media trolls

The despicable practice of social media trolling was highlighted in the previous section and it can be a vile and vindictive attack(s) on businesses or individuals. A simple Internet search will reveal a number of credible sources that provide numerous examples of trolling along with the consequences of such actions. In the UK Internet trolls are being targeted themselves by legal guidelines introduced by the Crown Prosecution Service (CPS). The act of trolling can now result in high court action leading to a maximum two years imprisonment for guilty offenders.

> *"The internet's not an anonymous place where people can post without any consequences. People should think about their own conduct. If you are grossly abusive to people, if you are bullying or harassing people online, then we will prosecute in the same way as if you did it offline"- Alison Saunders, Director of Public Prosecutions (BBC News, 2016).*

Returning to the soccer theme introduced in the previous section, one recent example of a trolling convictions saw a father and son each jailed for 12 months. Lewis Hawkins and his non-biological father David Riches created a bogus Twitter account and pretended to be a paedophile in order to troll the former soccer player Andy Woodward.

In a career spanning 20 years, based in the North of England, Woodward had played professional soccer for Crewe Alexandra, Bury and Sheffield United. It was in 2016 when he had become the first former footballer to waive his anonymity and go public about the sexual abuse scandal that has since rocked the soccer world. As a young trainee in the game, he had had to endure repeated sexual abuse. Since his initial revelation, more than 700 other former trainees had come forward with similar claims (Taylor, 2017).

When they set up the bogus Twitter account, using the identity "The Nonce", Hawkins and Riches had included a photograph of the man accused of abusing Woodward in the 1980s. The trolling had started only two days after Woodward had gone public on the sexual abuse scandal.

Trolling of this nature perpetrated by individuals who erroneously believe that Internet protects their anonymity is often intended to maximise the emotional distress and anxiety experienced by their victims. This was certainly achieved when Hawkins and Riches targeted Woodward who later remarked:

> *"The content of the messages horrified me to the point I felt dizzy. It made me feel sick. I dropped my phone on the table and I was in tears. I was home with my friends and family and virtually collapsed to the point where one of my family members had to hold me up from falling to the floor. Only two days before, I had given up my anonymity to speak publicly. I felt I had reverted to being a child and it took me back to tragic events. I was in a lot of fear. I felt vulnerable and powerless"* - *(Taylor, 2017).*

One very encouraging trend regarding Social Media trolling shows that convictions in the UK are on the rise. Statistics released by the Ministry of Justice shows that 1,501 defendants were prosecuted under the law in 2014, including 70 juveniles, while another 685 received a police caution. Of those convicted, 155 were jailed - compared to just seven a decade before. The average custodial sentence was 2.2 months (Telegraph, 2015).

4.12 Fake News

"A lie gets halfway around the world before the truth has a chance to get its pants on" – Winston Churchill

I was recently looking at some Facebook entries and noticed one posted on 17th January 2018 that was purporting to be an urgent warning. It was alerting readers to the fact that 'P-500 Paracetamol' must be avoided as the drug had been contaminated by the potentially deadly Machupo virus. On further investigation I found a number of Internet posts from twelve months earlier that seemed to confirm this warning but then from around April onwards of that year some credible Internet posts started to appear claiming that the warning was in fact a hoax.

Any initial panic that this fake albeit sensational news may have caused amongst paracetamol users could be understood as drugs have of course been contaminated before. Possibly one of the best known cases involved the pain killer Tylenol. In 1982, small quantities of the drug had been laced with potassium cyanide and seven people in the Chicago area died. The incident resulted in the introduction of tamper proof packaging by its manufacturer, Johnson & Johnson, which is still used today.

Making the distinction between genuine information and fake news also presents school and college students with a challenge when they are undertaking any research. Some advice on how to identify fake news has been included later in this book in section 5.1 - Social Media disrupts the classroom.

4.12.1 The Man Who Never Was

We have been hearing the expression 'Fake News' quite a lot in recent times especially since Donald Trump has come to political prominence. But contrary to what some may believe Trump did not invent the expression. History is full of examples of misinformation which was just another name for fake news.

One classic case occurred during World War II which the British named Operation Mincemeat and was later featured in the film "The Man that Never Was". The operation was designed to deceive the Axis powers into thinking that the intended 1943 Allied invasion of Sicily would take place elsewhere in the Mediterranean Sea. Such was the success of the operation that Hitler was allegedly convinced by the deception.

4.12.2 Arsenal invest £36 Million in teenage soccer sensation

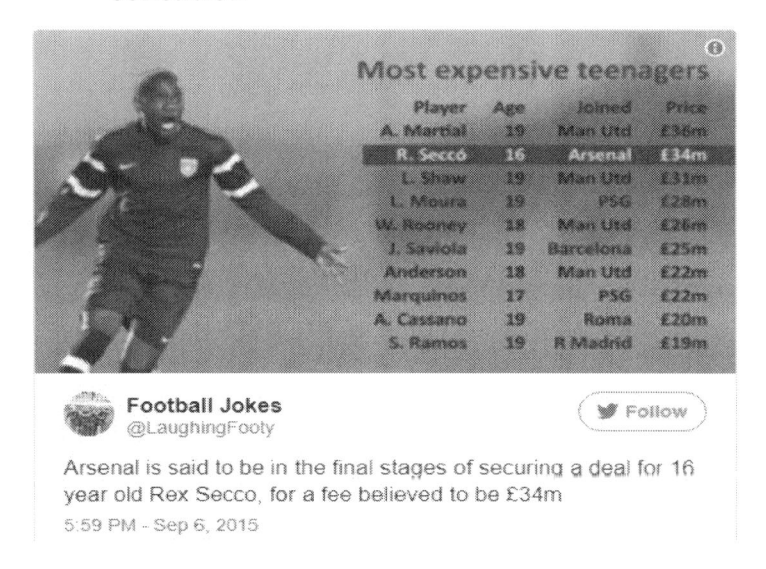

Figure 19: £36 million spent on teenage soccer sensation
Source: (Twitter, 2015)

This is not so much the tale of *'The Man who never was'* but of *'The Man that nobody has ever heard of'*. The story of Arsenal football club signing the unknown teenage soccer sensation Rex Secco went viral. However, close scrutiny of the Twitter identity should have warned readers that this was just a glorified wind-up. It was launched on the eve of the opening of the Soccerex Global Convention of 2015 having been orchestrated by the marketing agency Social Chain who intended to demonstrate the power of effective marketing on social media. Eagle eyed readers will have probably spotted that Rex Secco is in fact an anagram of 'Soccerex'. However, this caused much consternation amongst the North London club's fan base.

"While Gooners (nickname for Arsenal fans) may have been desperate for manager Arsene Wenger to spend big in the summer transfer window, splashing £34m on an unknown youngster may have been a bit much" - *(Oliver, 2015)*

4.12.3 The 2016 US Presidential Election

There is no truth filter, so if you rely on a stream of people's opinions and misinformation as your news source, it's not 100% reliable" - (Zoltick, 2018)

Moving on a year or so from the Rex Secco incident, the expression 'Fake News' has become virtually synonymous with Donald Trump. He has dismissed many 'news' stories as being fake and in some instances he may well have a point. In the final three months of the US presidential campaign, the top-performing fake election news stories on Facebook generated more engagement than the top stories from major credible news outlets such as the *New York Times*, *Washington Post* and the *Huffington Post*, etc. Below are some examples of fake news headlines that appeared during the 2016 US presidential campaign:

- "Pope backs Trump"

- "Ted Cruz's father killed JFK"

- "Hillary sold weapons to ISIS"

- "FBI agent suspected in Hillary Email leaks found dead"

- "Obama born in Kenya and not USA"

Apart from all going viral on Facebook in the run up to the election these fake headlines would all have been to the benefit of Donald Trump's presidential campaign because most denigrated his opponents. Sarah Katz is a former Facebook moderator whose job was to review complaints about inappropriate content that had been flagged by Facebook's users. Of the fake news issue she said on BBC Radio 5 Live's Emma Barnett Show:

> *"I think Facebook was caught out by fake news. In the run-up to the US election, it seemed highly off the radar"*
> – (Taylor, 2018)

These fake news posts gained such high engagement that BuzzFeed published an analysis on how they had outperformed real news on Facebook. During those critical months of the campaign, 20 top-performing false election stories from hoax sites and hyper partisan blogs generated nearly 9 million shares, reactions, and comments on Facebook alone. Within the same time period, the 20 best-performing election stories from 19 major news websites generated a total of just over 7 million shares, reactions, and comments on Facebook (Silverman, 2016).

Now in 2017, former US President Barack Obama has cautioned against the irresponsible use of social media, in a rare interview since stepping down in January. He warned that such actions were distorting people's understanding of complex issues, and spreading misinformation (BBC Radio 4, 2017).

But let us for a moment consider the point of publishing this fake news? Some items may be designed to score points over political opponents or to influence peoples' opinions. But more often than not, much of the fake news that gets published is deliberately sensationalised as it is intended to attract people to these websites in order to generate an income stream for the site owner. While visiting anyone of those websites, if you happen to click on an advert you will generate income for the website's owner by supporting their affiliate marketing programmes. The more sensational the news appears to be, the more likely it is that people will visit these websites

> *"The need for vigilance in distinguishing real journalism from "fake news" has become well established since Donald Trump was elected with help from bogus online stories." - (Swaine, 2017)*

But one story that is reluctant to go away — did the Russian's interfere with the 2016 US Presidential elections. Moreover, was there any collusion between the Russians and Donald Trump's team?

> *"Facebook says likely Russia-based group paid for political ads during US election" - (Solon, 2016)*

Former FBI Director Robert Mueller has been conducting an investigation into the allegations of Russian meddling. As a consequence, thirteen Russians have been charged with interfering in the US 2016 election, in a major development in the FBI investigation. Three of those named have also been accused of conspiracy to commit wire fraud and five have been accused of aggravated identity theft. Three Russian companies are also named in the indictment. One of them is the Internet Research Agency, based in St Petersburg, which the 37-page indictment said "*had a strategic goal to sow discord in the US political system, including the 2016 US presidential election*". Speaking at a news conference, Deputy Attorney General Rod Rosenstein said there was no allegation that any American was "a knowing participant in this illegal activity" nor was it alleged that the meddling altered the election outcome. The Russians also spent thousands of dollars a month buying political advertising and posted political messages on social media accounts that impersonated real US citizens (BBC - US & Canada News, 2018).

US media have also reported Mueller is investigating Mr Trump for possible obstruction of justice, both in the firing of FBI Director James Comey and whether Mr Trump tried to end an inquiry into sacked national security adviser Michael Flynn. All that said, US intelligence agencies have already concluded that Moscow tried to sway the presidential election in favour of Mr Trump (BBC News, 2017).

Ràndy Käus @RandyKaus · Jan 21

#Trump believes media lied about the size of his #Inauguration crowd. He also believes #Obama is from #Kenya & #TedCruz's father killed #JFK

2009   2017

♡   ⬆ 3   ♡ 3   ✉

Figure 20: Crowd size comparisons at Obama's and Trumps inaugurations
Source: Twitter

Randy Kaus posted the tweet illustrated in Figure 20 comparing the size of the crowds at Barack Obama's 2009 and Donald Trump 2017 inaugurations. Trump complained bitterly that the media was lying about the size of the crowds. However, in his defence I have to say without any meaningful timestamps included in the images, the comparisons are inconclusive. For example, the 2009 shot may have been taken as the inauguration started whereas the 2017 may have been several hours before it commenced. Maybe Trump and his team missed a trick here. They could have firmly repudiated Kaus's comparison by publishing an alternative photograph that supported Trump's version of events.

4.12.4 That green liquid contains cyanide, doesn't it?

It was April 12th, 2011 at Mriehel industrial estate in the Mediterranean island republic of Malta. A producer of domestic and industrial detergents, Drop Chemicals Limited experienced a serious fire that ultimately gutted their premises. Surprisingly, despite being several years after the arrival of Twitter and Facebook, the primary record of this event was videos uploaded to YouTube. The Maltese television news covered the fire although the commentary is in Maltese. But what should have been a business-as-usual fire and rescue mission was ultimately turned into a far bigger crisis by social media.

This was a multi-occupancy building which Drop Chemicals shared with a number of other high profile Maltese companies including the Bank of Valletta, Deloitte, the Malta Gaming Authority and the domestic appliances retailer Forestals. Clouds of black smoke billowed from the building and on their arrival the local fire and rescue service, known locally as the Civil Protection Department (CPD), ordered a complete evacuation of the remainder of the building. An exclusion zone of 200 metres was also set up and the public who lived in the immediate vicinity were advised to keep doors and windows shut (Callega, 2011).

Fortunately, no one was injured during this incident but this was perhaps more by good luck than good crisis management planning. However, two other serious issues did come to light.

- Firstly, some people trying to evacuate from the premises of the other companies that shared the building found their emergency exist routes obstructed. Their egress route took them through the premises of other companies and it transpired that some exits had been blocked off. Fortunately those individuals who had found themselves trapped ultimately did manage to find alternative exists. Had a building evacuation rehearsal been held, this potentially life threatening anomaly should have been discovered. However, there was no record found of any such exercises ever being conducted.
- The other big issue that came to light was caused by a reporter irresponsibility tweeting that the green liquid witnessed flowing out of the burning building was cyanide. Despite substantially increasing the overall level of concern still further amongst the CPD and local inhabitants, the reporter was clearly just creating a story that included a large helping of sensationalism. As it happens, the green liquid turned out to be nothing more sinister than washing-up liquid. This was hardly surprising as washing up liquid is one of Drop Chemicals primary products.

This is an example where social media, albeit in its infancy in Malta, was used to create a negative reaction through inaccurate speculation which was in effect fake news.

4.12.5 Fake blood appeal after 2017 Manchester bombing

"Queues have formed outside Manchester blood banks this morning - but the National Health Service Blood and Transplant Service is asking people to stay away and book a later appointment instead" - (Heward, 2017)

Following the bombing at the Manchester Arena after the 2017 Ariana Grande concert, appeals for blood donors were circulating on social media. However, the Manchester Evening News was able to report that these appeals did not originate from the UK's National Health Service (NHS). The NHS said that it had sufficient stocks to treat all patients but did not have the resources to cope with an influx of new donors in the immediate aftermath of the bombing.

What is unclear is whether this appeal was started by some well-meaning citizen who thought their actions might help or was it just a prankster at work.

Interestingly, four years earlier Simon Rickets of the Guardian was reporting on the 2013 Boston Marathon bombing and made an observation which seems very relevant to this section:

"Blood donors were needed. People need to give blood. This tweet is a regular when any disaster happens. It's nearly always not true, but to press "retweet" on this one feels like a civic duty" - (Ricketts, 2013)

4.13 Crowd funding after Manchester bombing

Moving on from the fake social media postings requesting blood donations after the Manchester Arena bombing, the power of the Internet was harnessed in a massive crowd funding appeal. Organised by the Manchester Evening News in partnership with the British Red Cross, three months after the suicide attack, by the 30th August 2017, the fund had reached £2,587,667 sterling. The intended beneficiaries were the victims of the bombing and their families (JustGiving, 2017).

4.14 Has social media saved lives?

It is unquestionably difficult to quantify the actual number of people that owe their lives to social media as this could be considered analytically subjective. Consequently, this section looks at a number of examples where it is believed credit for saving lives is appropriate. In some of the cases, just individuals were saved. In other instances perhaps hundreds or evens thousands survived because of social media.

4.14.1 Kenya Red Cross

Section 4.3 looked at the al Shabaab terrorist group live-tweeting while they attacked the Westgate shopping mall. During the attack, reporting for CNN, Daudi Khamadi Were suggested that the Kenyan Red Cross's performance on social media was far more effective than the Kenyan authorities. In addition to using its social media accounts to keep large groups of people informed on the Westgate crisis, the Red Cross also ran two successful campaigns:

It ran the biggest blood donation drive in Kenya's history which resulted in over 6,000 units of blood being donated within 48 hours of the start of the attack. Whenever a life threatening incident occurs around the world, an appeal for blood donations often follows. Unfortunately, it is not possible to quantify the number of actual lives saved but without the blood donations the final Westgate fatality count may well have been higher.

In conjunction with mobile phone operator Safaricom, The Kenyan Red Cross led a fund raising campaign for victims which had raised almost US$1.2 million within a week most of which was donated by individuals.

It also worth noting that in 2017 the Kenyan Red Cross used social media again to help highlight the plight of around 3 million Kenyans threatened by famine and who were in dire need of food aid. More than ten percent were seriously malnourished children. The crisis had been brought on by continuing drought conditions that were also affecting neighbouring Somalia and Ethiopia.

The Disasters Emergency Committee appeal, in which the Red Cross played an integral part, successfully raised £50 million sterling within 22 days (McVeigh & Rankin, 2017).

4.14.2 Hurricane Harvey - 2017

"Hurricane Harvey is the first major natural disaster of the social media age" – Nikki Usher, Media Professor, George Washington University, 2017

Perhaps Nikki Usher should have better qualified her quotation by mentioning that Harvey was the first major natural disaster experienced by the United States in the social media age. For example, some six years earlier in 2011 Japan had been struck by a massive earthquake measuring 8.9 on the Richter scale. Shortly afterwards a tsunami wave calculated to be 33 feet high

(10 m) came ashore penetrating up to six miles inland. There were many fatalities and much destruction including the swamping of the Fukushima Daiichi nuclear power station (Rafferty & Pletcher, 2011). Mobile phone carriers were limiting voice calls on heavily congested networks and some residents were unable to send SMS text messages too. But undeterred, people turned to social media and Twitter, Facebook and other social networking sites became an invaluable tool for millions of people caught up in the aftermath of the earthquake and tsunami (Wallop, 2011).

But the last time a major hurricane made landfall in the US had been in 2005 when Facebook was still in diapers and it was to be another twelve months before Twitter was even born. With wind speeds that reached up to 130 miles per hour (209 km/h), Hurricane Harvey made landfall in Texas between Port Aransas and Port O'Connor on 25th August 2017. In the vicinity of Houston alone, first responders struggled to deal with the deluge of emergency '911' calls with an estimated total of 56,000 over a fifteen hour period.

"We're finding out what a major flood emergency looks like in the era of social media" – Brian Stelter @brianstelter, 2017.

Hundreds of stranded Texas residents sought help by posting on Facebook and Twitter as Harvey swept across the state. They tweeted their addresses to emergency officials. They organised rescue missions through Facebook groups. And they posted harrowing pictures to emphasize just how high the flood waters were. Pleas for rescues were common such as: *"Anyone in North Houston have a boat and can rescue a 3 & 6 year old, mom, gramma and grandpa and 2 dogs*?" Web-enabled emergency responses have been seen in other countries before, but never in the United States on this scale (CNN Media, 2017).

With 911 emergency despatchers not always able to respond owing to the sheer volume of calls, like the Japanese earthquake and tsunami victims of 2011, Harvey's victims turned to Facebook and Twitter to seek help. Time cites the case of Maritza Willis who turned to her 400 plus Facebook friends and posted a call for help. She had two children and a sick teenager with her and the water around her was 'swallowing her up'. A little over an hour later, she tweeted that help had come her way. *"Got picked up by the fire rescue,"* Willis posted. *"Thank You. One of you had connections and all I can say is I'll be eternally grateful!!!"* - (Rhodan, 2017).

But despite the appeals for help via social media, Government Agencies were still instructing citizens to report Harvey related emergencies via 911:

 **U.S. Coast Guard** ☑
@USCG

To report a #harvey emergency you must call numbers below or 911 for assistance. If busy keep trying. Do not report distress on social media

The U.S. Coast Guard is conducting urban search and rescue in the city of Houston. If you are in need of rescue, call 911 or the U.S. Coast Guard Houston Command Center. Do not report your information on social media sites.
Sector Houston Command Center numbers:
281-464-4851
281-464-4852
281-464-4853
281-464-4854
281-464-4855

Stay calm, do not panic.
Do not go into the attic, rescuers from the air cannot see you.
Get to high ground immediately.
Mark the roof to be seen from the air. Wave sheets, towels, to be noticed from the air.

5:04 PM - 27 Aug 2017

4,766 Retweets **3,290** Likes

💬 168   🔁 4.8K   ♡ 3.3K   ✉

Figure 21: Texas citizens instructed not to use social media
Source: (Gilmer, 2017).

It would appear that government agencies were simply not ready to cope with managing a disaster of this nature using social media. Even so, social media has proved itself to be a positive force in flooded Texas (Gilmer, 2017).

But one additional and not necessarily welcome challenge that social media will have presented despatchers and first responders is not just the pleas for help posted on the likes of Facebook and Twitter but the volume of shared and retweeted posts that could potentially grow exponentially. This has the capability of causing serious information overload as especially as well-meaning citizens could be unwittingly reposting information about victims who have already been rescued.

In 2005, Hurricane Katrina killed more than eighteen hundred souls while the death toll for Harvey stands at less than one hundred. Exactly how many lives were saved is impossible to say. However, it does seem that many of Harvey's victims have social media to thank for their rescue especially with 911 despatchers struggling to manage the deluge of emergency calls that they faced.

4.14.3 Stranded Indian workers faced starvation

July 2016 witnessed a humanitarian crisis in the making in Saudi Arabia where in excess of 10,000 Indian workers had been laid-off due to global drop in the price of oil. Many had not been paid for several months and money to purchase food was running out.

The Indian External Affairs minister, Sushma Swaraj, appealed on Twitter to the 3 million strong Indian community in the country to "help your brothers and sisters". She also vowed that no Indian worker rendered unemployed would go without food. Her initial response came following a tweet by a man who said around 800 Indians in Jeddah were starving having not eaten for the last three days and he sought her intervention although she later reported that the actual number was in the order of 10,000 (NDTV, 2016).

In response, the Indian consulate in Jeddah said it had distributed more than 15,000kg (34,000lb) of food on one day alone, with the help of Indian nationals in the city. Meantime, an airlift was being prepared to repatriate the unemployed Indian citizens from Saudi Arabia (BBC Middle East, 2016).

Figure 22: Sushma Swaraj's Twitter commitment
Source: Twitter

4.14.4 Just to let you know, I'm safe !

Facebook has a feature which it calls its 'Safety Check'. So what is it exactly? Safety Check allows people to quickly share that they're safe with friends and family and helps them connect with people they care about. During a disaster, Safety Check will help you:

- Let friends and family know you're safe

- Check on friends and family in the affected area and connect with them
- Share what you know about a friend or family member's status

Source: (Facebook, 2018)

In On April 25th 2015, measuring 7.8 on the Richter scale, Nepal experienced its worst earthquake in more than 80 years. The devastated area was struck by a second earthquake 17 days later this time with a magnitude of 7.3. There were slightly less than 9,000 fatalities and over 20,000 were injured mostly by the original quake. Facebook activated its Safety Check feature which helped friends and families locate their nearest and dearest. By using Safety Check, users close to the site of the disaster were able to flag themselves safe and notify their friends. Besides this, Safety Check also urges other users to indicate when people they know are safe. The feature was developed by Facebook after its engineers in Japan developed the Disaster Message Board to help people make contact during and after the 2011 Tohoku earthquake and tsunami (Mercy Corps, 2015).

4.14.5 Injured biker rescued by Twitter

As she flew over the handlebars of her mountain bike, seconds before slamming into the ground, Leigh Fazzina remembers thinking to herself: "I'm going to break my neck. And there is no one out here to help me" - (Huffington Post, 2010)

Healthcare PR and social media communications pro Leigh Fazzina was thankful for Twitter when she suffered a serious bike accident while taking part in a mini-triathlon in Farmington, Connecticut. Following the accident, with a mobile signal that was too weak to make a call, Leigh turned to Twitter to alert her followers to her plight saying "I've had a serious injury and NEED Help! Can someone please call Winding Trails in Farmington, CT and tell them I'm stuck because I have had a bike crash in the woods." Within seconds, Fazzina's Twitter followers and colleagues from all over the country notified authorities. The Farmington Police Department received a call from a woman in California, who guided rescuers to Winding Trails. Fazzina continued to tweet landmarks and directions. Twenty minutes later, she reported that she heard sirens and hoped rescuers would be able to locate her. Even after her rescue, she remained in contact with her Twitter followers, letting them know she was safe and even recording a video of the rescue (Donnelly, 2010).

4.14.6 Kawasaki disease diagnosed on Facebook

The UK's National Health Service explains that Kawasaki disease is a rare condition that mainly affects children under the age of five. It's also known as mucocutaneous lymph node syndrome. The characteristic symptoms are a high temperature that lasts for more than five days, with:

- a rash
- swollen glands in the neck
- dry, cracked lips
- red fingers or toes
- red eyes

After a few weeks the symptoms become less severe, but may last longer. At this stage, the affected child may have peeling skin on their fingers and toes. However, up to 5% of children with Kawasaki disease experience complications with their heart. Complications can be fatal in about 1% of cases (NHS, 2018).

In 2015, Deborah Kogan posted a photograph on Facebook of her son Leo's rash which was initially diagnosed as a Streptococcal infection. But his condition deteriorated and his face became very badly swollen so Deborah posted a second photo 24 hours later. Leo's condition turned out to be Kawasaki disease and a friend who recognised the condition from the Facebook post phoned Deborah and strongly urged her to take little Leo straight to hospital. Other Facebook friends also contacted Deborah having reached similar conclusions.

The Washington Post reported that Leo had been admitted to hospital for treatment and was discharged after three weeks. Although his liver was recovering from the disease and his heart had mostly healed, he will have to undergo echocardiograms annually for the remainder of his life. His mother Deborah acknowledged that "my son could suddenly drop dead of a heart attack" - (Flock, 2011)

4.14.7 Sadly social media couldn't help this time

"Rob Williams, one of Britain's leading young entrepreneurs, has fallen 60ft to his death on a snowboarding holiday, in a tragedy played out live on social networking website Twitter" - (Edwards, 2009)

Twenty-nine year old Rob Williams died after he and business partner, Jason Tavaria, who together run a multi-million pound music firm, became separated from their party during a blizzard at the Swiss resort of Verbier, while on a trip with Michelle Dewberry, the winner of BBC television reality show the Apprentice.

Urgent appeals were posted by her on the Twitter website and Mr Tavaria, also 29, sent his friends and rescue teams a GPS satellite navigation signal from his iPhone, which pinpointed his location. He was rescued six hours later.

Mr Williams, however, had fallen 66ft down a cliff on to rocks below and due to the "white-out" conditions, a rescue helicopter could not be scrambled. Search teams on foot found him seven hours after he had gone missing, by which time the businessman had died in the freezing conditions (Edwards, 2009).

4.15 We are all human

"To err is human, but to really foul things up you need a computer (or a smart phone or a tablet.......)"

Here is a small selection of examples of some inappropriate pressing of the wrong buttons while the world looked on. Fortunately, apart from some understandably extremely concerned Hawaii residents, none of the incidents resulted in a major crisis but are more likely to have caused some rather embarrassing egg-on-face moments.

4.15.1 A *'plane'* mistake to make

"British Airways accidentally recommends its Facebook followers to fly with big rivals Virgin Atlantic in embarrassing social media mix-up" - *(Mallinson, 2016)*

Was this a simple accident or a case of insider threat? Either way a great many people had a laugh at British Airways expense and it was not so much a crisis but really nothing more than a storm in a teacup.

The story goes that Virgin Atlantic posted an advertisement on its Facebook page pointing out that there has never been a better time to visit London. But, whoops, it looks like someone in the British Airways' social media team was having a bad day at the office and managed to share its rival's posting. This hilarious faux-pas did not go unnoticed by BA's customers many of whom left comments about BA advertising on behalf of its competitor such as - *"Did someone click the share post button by mistake"*, *"Trying to get rid of some customers"* and *"I think someone's getting fired"*.

British Airways shared Virgin Atlantic's post.
19 mins ·

Virgin Atlantic
October 19 at 6:07pm ·

There's never been a better time to visit London. Book today with Virgin Atlantic

Take an eye opening trip
Fly nonstop in comfort and style to your next adventure in London with Virgin Atlantic

VIRGIN-ATLANTIC.COM

Book Now

Figure 23: BA accidentally shares Virgin Atlantic's posting
Source: Facebook

In the end, this seemed to conclude as light hearted banter between rivals. While it is not clear whether or not heads rolled over at BA, Virgin certainly appreciated the gesture and responded by thanking BA for sharing its post. They also added the hashtag *"#onethingweagreeon"* is that it's a good time to go to London except we differ on how to get there.

4.15.2 Whoops – "Wrong button" says Minister

Following the UK cabinet reshuffle on 8th January 2018, the Health Secretary Jeremy Hunt erroneously pressed the 'like' button on the tweet announcing that the former Education Secretary Justine Greening had resigned from the cabinet. However, an embarrassed Mr Hunt later tweeted:

Figure 24: Minister presses wrong button
Source: (Twitter, 2018)

4.15.3 Take cover - Incoming !!

An incoming missile alert caused panic in Hawaii on 13th January 2018 before it was declared to be a false alarm some 18 minutes after the original alarm was raised. The warning had been sent to mobile phone users who received a message saying:

"Ballistic missile threat inbound to Hawaii. Seek immediate shelter. This is not a drill."

The message was also broadcast on television and radio. The State Governor David Ige apologised to residents explaining that an employee had 'pressed the wrong button'.

While there was no report of social media being used during the actual alert process, Twitter was used by @Hawaii_EMA to inform followers of the false alert (BBC News, 2018).

4.16 Is social media having its very own crisis?

With a growing number of social media platforms competing for our patronage, like any other business it is inevitable that some will be successful while others will not. In fact over 40 platforms have either closed down or have merged with another site and more than half of these 'failures' have occurred within the last 5 years. Conversely, there is no doubt Facebook has become the most popular site to date although many millennials are now leaving in their droves. The Financial Times suggested that Facebook fatigue is the root cause while others cite the ever growing number of grey haired users as not being 'cool'. As one 20 year old woman remarked *"It's like going to a friend's house for a party and finding your Mother is there too. It's just a complete turn-off"*. That said, with an estimated 2 billion users, there is probably very little chance of Facebook joining the failed social media site statistics any time soon.

However, evidence of social media's fragility has been revealed when instead of delivering the news, it became the news. On 21st February 2018, reality TV personality Kylie Jenner tweeted the question: *"Sooo does anyone else not open Snapchat anymore? Or is it just me?"* The impact on the share price of Snapchat's parent company Snap was immediate and devastating with an estimated $1.3 billion being wiped of the company's value.

Any company, social media or otherwise, would love to be able to claim the patronage of such high profile individuals amongst their clientele. However, when one of them turns round and so publically makes such damaging remarks, in this day and age it is often social media that is the bearer of such bad news. We can of course argue that this is just an example of adverse publicity. Even so, the irony is that by just asking that question Kylie Jenner created a crisis for Snapchat by potentially undermining its credibility and popularity making it the news and costing the company dearly. Watch this space !

5 Massive negative impact seen in education

There have been occasions when I been delivering training for companies and also in my capacity as a part time university lecturer when I have frequently observed students who would rather play with their smart phones than pay attention. Some might plead mitigating circumstances as they were just taking down lecture notes on a tablet rather than using pen and paper. Fair enough but there are many who would rather commune with social media than participate in the subject being taught. I have to be up front and admit that I do find this practice bad mannered and irritating but it is a sign of the times we live in. Having also spoken with colleagues, I know that it is a common problem – a situation that has been deteriorating across the education sector for a number of years now. However, the reality is that this apparent student inattentiveness it is just the tip of a very large and worrying iceberg.

In my case, university students that I am delivering to have paid to be educated but if they choose to spend their time more focused on social media than the lecture content, that's their call. However, if a company has paid me as a consultant to train its employees, then I do have an issue with attendees playing with social media rather than being attentive because the client will not be getting full value for money. Before commencing the delivery, I endeavour to seek guidance from the training sponsor regarding the company's policy on use of smart phones during training – are they allowed, frowned upon or even banned all together? Depending on their response, I will manage it accordingly. There are a number of *'turn your phone off'* videos posted on YouTube that can be used to help get the message across. Personally I like the Star Wars video where the character Darth Vader comes close to throttling someone who takes a personal call at a most inappropriate time.

Schools and colleges can of course implement rules and regulations concerning the use of phones and social media within their premises. There are those which have identified specific windows when they can be used (e.g. breaks and lunchtimes etc.) while others have banned them all together from the campus. It also well within the right of schools and colleges to ban the use of its computers to access social media sites. Moreover, should they choose to do so, it is also technically possible to block access to predetermined sites from their computers and networks.

All that said, perhaps this is where I may seem to contradict myself as there have been occasions when I have actually encouraged students to use their smart devices during a lecture. But and this is a big 'but' this has been to allow them to utilise it as a tool usually during break-out team exercises. I feel this can help to enhance their appreciation of how their studies can benefit from social media rather than just using it as a plaything that they feel they have to pander to whenever and where ever it demands their attention. One thing I do believe is important that people involved in education at all levels need to figure out how to successfully harness social media in the classroom for the benefit of their students.

5.1 Social Media disrupts the classroom

"Social media can wreak havoc when students become distracted in the middle of class. Some educators have gone so far as to ban social media in the classroom, but others says that learning to control social media is part of the learning process and the benefits outweigh the negatives" - (Kapko, 2014)

To date, the growing consensus within education circles is that social media is having a negative impact on the classroom. Recent research has found that in secondary schools, pupils accessing social media with their smart devices can cause as much as 11 days' lost teaching time each year per teacher. In an academic year of 39 weeks, that presents around 6% of teaching time during the school year.

The disruptions themselves come in many different forms. Almost half (46%) of secondary school teachers have experienced pupils using social media smartphone apps during classes, while four in 10 (40%) have experienced pupils' confidence being damaged by social media issues. Meanwhile, over one quarter (27%) have experienced social media cyber bullying in class and 17% have had pupils sharing explicit or pornographic content. Half of teachers (50%) say that social media issues such as these are contributing to their pupils achieving lower grades than they could (Vickers, 2017).

To add further to Vickers' findings, Whitman claims that ninety-two percent of teens browse the internet daily and 24 percent report they are "online constantly" (Whitman, 2016). This implies that 1 in 4 of all teenagers are permanently online even in the classroom.

> *"There are four primary cons that arise from the use of social media in the classroom: distraction, academic dishonesty (or cheating), discerning fact from fiction and cyberbullying" - Scott Silverman, Associate Director of Student Affairs, University of California (Kapko, 2014)*

Focusing on cyber bulling and a little lower than Vickers' survey findings has been in Australia where one in five children say they experienced bulling within the previous 12 months. In worst case scenarios this has even led to suicide. In one high profile incident, fourteen year old Amy "Dolly" Everett, the face of the iconic Akubra Australian outback hat took her own life "to escape the evil in this world" (BBC News, 2018).

In the UK the National Society for the Prevention of Cruelty to Children (NSPCC) says that they have no idea about the number of children who are affected by online abuse. However, in 2015/16 the NSPCC recorded 4,541 counselling sessions with young people who cited cyberbullying as their main concern which was an increase of 13% on the previous year.

"Young people described malicious and hurtful messages being posted about them on their profiles, blogs, online pictures or posts. The negative messages ranged from bullying and abusive comments about how the young person looked, to directly telling the young person they should go and kill themselves" - (Childline, 2016, p. 7)

The NSPCC have also established that cyber bullying not only affects academic performance, but it encourages absenteeism amongst its victims and is linked to mental and physical health problems. In a quarter of counselling sessions about bullying, children also talked about mental health and wellbeing issues (NSPCC - London, 2016).

In an effort to escape cyber bullying, an ABC News study also established that many students stay away from school. In the region of 500 US schools were involved in the study and the conclusion reached estimated that circa 160,000 students across the country are absent every day because of bullying (Whitman, 2016).

Silverman also identifies discerning fact from fiction as a challenge for students. This of course reiterates some of the concerns raised in the earlier section about Fake News. However, there are some pilot initiatives being set up to make it easier for both students and the public to spot fake news. In the UK in December 2017, the BBC announced that, following a year-long study with Salford University, they would be running a pilot project where up to 1,000 schools will be invited to participate. James Harding, the director of BBC News, said:

> *"This is an attempt to go into schools to speak to young people and give them the equipment they need to distinguish between what's true and what's false." - (BBC Entertainment and Arts, 2017)*

Meanwhile, in recognition of Donald Trump's popularisation of the expression 'Fake News', the Open University plans to publish a series of YouTube videos on the first anniversary of his inauguration. These will be designed to assist the general public in making more informed decisions regarding the authenticity of news items (Burns, 2017).

From the University of Sheffield comes the offer of a free course on the *Future Learn* platform on how to spot misleading statistics. Entitled *"Making sense of data in the media"*, it helps people establish what numbers published by the media can be trusted and what is fake news (Future Learn, 2018).

The last of Silverman's points to consider in this section is what he refers to as academic dishonesty (or cheating) – sometimes called plagiarism. This is primarily about taking other people's work in whatever form it may be without acknowledging the original source and passing it off as your own.

> *Has the ubiquity of social media given plagiarism new life? - (Taras, 2017)*

To help recognise instances of plagiarism there are technical solutions available such as *Turnitin* and *Unicheck.* However, in the ideal world it is better to discourage plagiarism in the first place rather than have to deal with it after the event.

> *"Sixty-eight percent of college students admit to 'cutting and pasting material from the Internet without citation'" - (Blum, 2010)*

In addition to using plagiarism checkers, Taras also identifies five other points which are directed more at prevention rather dealing with the aftermath:

- Structure student assignments so they will necessitate quick Google search.

- Address the ethics of plagiarism ensuring that students comprehend why it's wrong and how it could have a detrimental effect on them and their education.
- Ensure they appreciate the difference between copying, citing, quoting and plagiarism.
- Make your deadlines realistic as a common cause of plagiarism is a heavy academic load leaving students believing they have insufficient time to complete their assignments.
- Teach older students how to thoroughly research a topic

Source: (Taras, 2017).

5.2 Would adding social media to the curriculum help?

Contrary to what its critics may think, in the longer term social media offers anything but a dead-end career. In fact, in its relatively short existence, it has shown that it is a dynamic field that is constantly growing and evolving while responding to new technologies and platforms. So should social media be taught in schools? I have certainly found a number of recommendations which in some cases date back several years strongly suggesting that social media needs to be added to school curriculums. With respect to tertiary options, there are a number of universities that have included social media offerings in their prospectuses but students will have invariably reached their late teens or beyond by the time they attain this level of academia. In my view, social media education should be available to children at a much earlier age. However, try as I may, I can find very little evidence of the subject of social media in all its multi-faceted forms actually being taught in schools that cater for pre-university aged students.

> *"It's clear that there's still work to do when it comes to protecting young people online, and ensuring the internet is a force for good" – Russell Haworth, CEO, Nominet (Rogers, 2017)*

If I was defining a strategy, in the first instance I would target 5 to 11 year old children. In the UK children are encouraged to be mindful of what is referred to as *'stranger-danger'*. The expression's widespread usage is intended to be a warning that strangers could present a real threat to individual children. But to work, this naturally depends upon a visual observation by a child. However, the darker side of social media can be associated with the dangers of bullying, sexting (e.g. using social media to send messages or images of a sexually explicit nature etc.) and grooming have become widespread. Contrary to the *'stranger-danger'* warnings, a child can be groomed on social media by person or persons unseen.

While, bullying has been around for ever and is not just confined to the school playground, social media has provided an alternative means for bullies to torment their targeted individuals. Despite a school of thought that social media spawned sexting its origins can actually be traced back many thousands of years. Likewise, grooming is also nothing new but social media has taken them both to a completely new level making it far easier for perpetrators. The UK charity Child Line explains that anyone can groom someone. A 'groomer' is someone who makes an emotional connection with someone to try and make them do things like:

- have sexual conversations online or by text messages
- send naked images of yourself, which is sometimes called sexting
- send sexual videos of yourself
- do something sexual live on webcam
- meet up with them in person.

They might be old, or young and they can be male or female (Childline, 2017).

At the very least, 5 to 11 year olds should be taught to understand these online dangers, how to recognise the signs of grooming and comprehend how they should be behave should they have the misfortune to be confronted by a groomer. A Nominet survey also shows that most teachers seem to agree, as three-quarters (75%) of those surveyed think that social media etiquette and safety should be taught during school (Rogers, 2017). The UK's National Society for the Prevention of Cruelty to Children (NSPCC) has long campaigned for legislation to be introduced that better protects children. The new offence of sexual communication with a child was introduced on 3rd April 2017. Previously, until a groomer attempted to meet their targets, police were powerless to intervene. The NSPCC stated that in the six months following the introduction of the new offence, a staggering 1,316 cases of grooming were recorded in the UK (BBC News, 2018). The NSPCC has also called for social media platforms to flag up potential cases of grooming especially as the technology needed to achieve this already exists. As of January 2018, Facebook has announced it is already using the technology to that end.

I can also see a place for offering social media studies to secondary school pupils. However, to try and teach 11 year olds and upwards how to use social media from a purely personal perspective, to borrow an old English expression, would be akin to *'teaching your grandmother to suck eggs'*. They will have long since become digital natives! Even so, the opportunity would be there to harness their self-developed skill and experience while guiding them in building and maintaining their own mature and respectable digital profiles.

The importance of impressing upon students the rights and wrongs that should be observed when engaging with social media activity cannot be understated as the lack of a sound moral compass could come back to haunt them later in life. In 2017 at least 10 students previously accepted to Harvard had their offers rescinded after administrators discovered offensive posts in a private, online Facebook messaging group. The Holocaust, child abuse, sexual assault, racism as well as posts that denigrated minority groups, were all fair game in the meme-focused private chat group. While Harvard does not comment on individual applicants' admission statuses, incoming students are explicitly told upon receiving an offer that behaviour that brings into question their moral character can jeopardize their admission - (Heilweil, 2017).

> *"If schools taught a class on social media, and that was the only class students took, some could still find employment monitoring feeds, creating snapchats, producing vines, or curating Pinterest for a business. Businesses will pay for these services"* - (Green, 2015(b)).

Those who wish to pursue the subject further could be focused towards the use of social media in a business context. This could include areas such as optimising the use of platforms like Facebook, Twitter, Instagram and YouTube to generate and raise product and service profiles. This would go hand-in-hand with engaging with user communities while promoting brand awareness and increasing market share. While it may not prove to have the same level of box office attraction as other aspects of social media, let's not forget the very topic of this book – managing social media in a crisis. I would like to think that within the not too distant future it will be possible to select social media as an optional subject to study with the possibility of leaving school with a meaningful qualification.

But here is an analogy that considers the downside of teaching social media in schools. I can remember back in the 1980's my now grown-up son playing with his Spectrum 128 +3 computer – something which has long since been a museum piece. He can have been no more than about eight years old at the time when a visiting aged aunt asked him what he was doing. Very articulately he explained what he was up to but then incredibly diplomatically for one so young added that she probably wouldn't understand as she was 'old'. The irony is that there is a parallel with social media which many consider it to be primarily the domain of the millennials. To reiterate, they are the digital natives. Consequently, in all probability the students may well know more about the subject than their teachers.

5.3 Threats of violence at schools including shootings

In 2012, a 19 year old Maryland student was arrested after posting death threats to the Reddit forum as well as making anonymous voice and video postings to the chat site Omegle.com. The arrest came after other users of the social media sites alerted the authorities. According to his posts, Alexander Song intended to *"kill enough people to make to the national news"*. Police traced him via his IP address which was provided by Reddit although when he was detained, police found no evidence of any weapons (Pan, 2012).

Winding forward to October 2017, it was reported that both schools and local police in North West Florida were closely monitoring social media. This followed pupils making threats of violence at Navarre High School and Fort Walton Beach which was reported to the schools by both worried students and their parents. The proliferation of threats resulting from sharing posts can also result in students staying at home for several days after the threat with some literally fearing for their lives.

"A student posted to Instagram referencing certain cliques, saying 'I hope you all have fun in hell because

I'm going to drag you down with me.' That student was suspended as a result of the post" - (Kennedy, 2017)

One student was arrested and charged with having used another students Snapchat account to send a threat to injure or kill. The implication was that he intended to *'shoot up the school'*. With a growing history of school and college shooting incidents especially in the USA, threats of this nature are being taken seriously.

Chief Assistant Florida State Attorney Greg Marcille said that:

"Juveniles make up almost all of the school threat-related cases prosecuted by the state. While the majority of those threats are made via platforms like Facebook, Instagram or Snapchat, Florida laws address only "verbal or written communications," which can complicate the prosecution of those cases" - (Kennedy, 2017).

Schools and colleges find themselves in a very difficult situation. Firstly not all would necessarily have the resources, either from a critical mass perspective or a social media skillset capability, to track and deal with any threats that have been posted. Second, making a balanced judgment call on what could be a problematical decision to make vis-à-vis what to tell students and parents and what to withhold as their goal should be to inform rather than create mass hysteria. Clearly, without knowing whether the students are having a joke or whether they have the means and the intent to go through with a threat, until proven otherwise, every threat needs to be taken seriously. One thing is certainly clear is that like Navarre High

School and Fort Walton Beach mentioned earlier, all schools and colleges must work closely with the law enforcement agencies and avoid working in isolation.

5.4 When will it end?

The draft of this book was being proof read and I thought I had finished adding content. However, I felt that I needed to include this extra section to reflect upon a tragic event that was unfolding in front of me in real time. On 14th February 2018; via social media I witnessed a live active shooter incident while in progress. I first picked up traffic on Twitter coming from Coral Springs Police (@CoralSpringsPD) in Florida but that was primarily retweeting posts from the Broward Sheriff's Office (@browardsheriff). Both referred to the hashtag *#stonemanshooting*.

> *"It's catastrophic. There really are no words."* - Sheriff Scott Israel

The active shooter incident occurred at Marjory Stoneman Douglas High school in Parkland which is located to the north of Miami. The attack was perpetrated by a lone gunman who was later taken into custody and identified as 19 year old Nikolas Cruz. He was a former pupil who had been expelled from the school the previous year for disciplinary reasons. As of 6 pm local time on the day of the shooting, Sheriff Scott Israel announced that 17 people were known to have lost their lives and a number of others were being treated in hospital for their injuries.

Unlike the other examples in section 5.3, on this occasion social media appears to have played only a minimal part leading up to this tragedy. While Sheriff Israel described Cruz's now deleted social media accounts as disturbing, they carried no indication that the shooting would happen. Neither had Cruz given any other kind of warning of what he intended to do. However, he had previously posted a comment on YouTube stating that he saw himself as a 'professional school shooter'. The FBI confirmed that they had previously received a tip off about the post but admitted that they had not properly followed up on the warning. This active shooter incident was at least the 18th in the US this year on or around school premises according to research by Everytown for Gun Safety. Since 2013, there have been 291 reported school shootings in America, which averages out to about one per week (BBC - US & Canada News, 2018).

Interviewed on BBC Breakfast television, Marjory Stoneman Douglas High school teacher Ivy Schamis, explained that she was teaching a class of seniors when they first heard the shooting outside in the hallway.

> *"The kids just instantaneously dove for the floor. They didn't think about it. They didn't question it they just tried to take cover around the perimeter of the classroom"* – Ivy Schamis, 2018

Cruz shot out the glass panel in the door hitting several of the students inside the classroom two of whom were fatality wounded. However, he failed to gain access and moved on. The school had held active shooter practice drills so when confronted by this genuine threat, the students did exactly the right thing and sought cover as best they could. Schamis added that while there is an armed police officer assigned to the school, the campus is large and he clearly could not be everywhere (Schamis, 2018).

Student Lewis Mizen also spoke to BBC Breakfast television explaining that he was one of around twenty students who were crammed into a large closet for approximately 90 minutes before being rescued. Mizen explained that from inside the closet they had some idea about what was going on by following social media posts. But because there was so much information being posted they could not distinguish between what was true and what was just a rumour. One post even claimed that there were as many as five shooters (Mizen, 2018).

The importance of rehearsing for life threatening scenarios such as an active shooter cannot be understated. The way that Schamis's students reacted provides testament to the value of the lessons they had learned and they all demonstrated a level of unconscious competence. In other words they didn't need think about what they had to do, they didn't wait for instructions, they just reacted instinctively because of the training they had undertaken.

As for social media's involvement in this heartrending event, it can be broken into three parts – before, during and after the incident.

a. Activity was minimal before the shooting
b. During the attack we witnessed a rapid ramping up of the flow of information along with updates and comments. Students inside the school also took to social media including posting some graphic videos. But as has happened

with other crises in recent times, inaccurate rumours and misinformation was also circulating.

c. In the aftermath, as well as the outpouring of grief, the recriminations started.

- Why did the FBI not apprehend Cruz prior to the shooting
- What never seems to be far from the surface in the United States is the debate about the right to bear arms. So it is no surprise that social media has been hosting exchanges between supporters of the National Rifle Association and the anti-gun lobby.

While we may learn in time what motivated Nikolas Cruz to commit this despicable atrocity it won't bring back the dead nor will it offer any comfort to the bereaved. The various case studies in this book have highlighted the potentially malicious nature of social media's dark side. However, on this occasion I believe that it was nothing more than an innocent bystander that merely reported on what its users saw.

6   Is '*Big Brother*' watching us on social media too?

In 1949 George Orwell published his classic novel 'nineteen eighty four'. Often referred to simply as '1984', in his book he describes a futuristic dystopian society where critical thought is suppressed under a totalitarian regime. The book spawned the expression '*Big Brother is watching*' which is often used to refer to any ruler or government that invades the privacy of its citizens. The storyline finds *Big Brother* as the ruler of this dystopian society and his very survival depends upon the Thought Police (aka the secret police) and its use of surveillance and psychological monitoring techniques to identify and eliminate members of society who posed a threat to *Big Brother*.

Now in the 21st century, the presence of Closed-Circuit Television (CCTV) has become a way of life in today's developed world an evolution that is justified by some very strong arguments. There are those who would reason that it has become a necessary evil in modern society while others believe that CCTV is becoming ever more intrusive. In the United Kingdom, in 2011 the Daily Mail newspaper claimed that there is one camera for every thirty-two of the country's inhabitants. Moreover, on average every member of the UK population is recorded going about their business more than 300 times a day (Mail Online, 2011).

By 2016 it is believed that the ratio of CCTV cameras to UK inhabitants had dropped to as low as one camera for every ten inhabitants (CIA Fire and Security, 2016). While there are inevitably some who find the reality of an Orwellian *Big Brother* state watching their every move an unpalatable situation, arguably for honest citizens, CCTV's advantages far outweigh its disadvantages. Even so, it is hardly surprising that an organisation calling itself Big Brother Watch was set up in the UK in 2009 with its mission defined as ensuring that those who fail to respect our privacy, undermine our online security, or fail to protect our personal data, are held to account. They campaign on behalf of the individual to ensure their privacy and civil liberties are maintained in the digital age by government, public authorities and businesses. It also produces unique research exposing the misuse of powers, informative factsheets explaining complex laws, and briefings for parliament, the press and the public (Big Brother Watch, 2018).

In section 6.5 - Witness for the Prosecution and the Defence, there are examples of businesses using CCTV combined with social media to apprehend criminals. But are *Big Bother-esk* state sponsored organisations monitoring and acting upon social media entries and perhaps even subjecting posts to state censorship? On both counts, strong evidence exists that the answer is 'yes'.

We need to remind ourselves that much of what we put out there in social media land is in the public domain and can be just as easily seen by our families and friends as well as the police and security services. So do I personally have an issue with that? No, I do not although I would add one important caveat. If there is something that I consider to be of a personal nature that I would prefer not to broadcast then I just don't post it to Facebook or the like. I certainly would not rely upon the platforms privacy settings over good judgement concerning what to post and what not to post. Quite simply, if we do not like the idea of 'strangers' reading our social media posts, then just remember that no one is forcing you to use sites like Facebook or Twitter et al.

What might qualify as a 'stop press' item for this chapter was that Facebook recently announced that it plans to better manage the security of its members' identity by using facial recognition technology (Quiñonero Candela, 2017). However, I did find an interesting corresponding BBC article about a character called Jonathan Hirshon. He has more than 3,000 friends on Facebook and regularly updates his profile with personal information - where he is going on holiday, what he has cooked for dinner and the state of his health. But what he has never shared on the social network, or anywhere else online, is a picture of himself (Wakefield, 2017). So perhaps Jonathan Hirshon won't be in any rush to use this new facial recognition facility but I am sure that Big Brother and his cohort won't be slow in taking full advantage of any subsequent benefits that might come their way.

Finally, when it comes to social media censorship which does exist in certain countries, in my view that is a different matter entirely and it would certainly fit well within the Orwellian society that I mentioned earlier. I will be talking more about censorship in section 6.2.

6.1 Social media intercept prevents terrorist attack

As I was writing this chapter my attention was caught by two BBC television news reports, albeit on different days, about how authorities had apprehended would-be terrorists that were planning to commit atrocities. In the first case, the FBI apprehended a former US Marine, Everitt Aaron Jameson, who was planning a terrorist attack. Apparently, his intended target was the popular tourist area in San Francisco known as Pier 39.

It would seem that Jameson was acting as a lone wolf - the type of terrorist that can be notoriously difficult for security services to detect. However, it was his social media activity that brought him to the attention of the FBI having expressed support for "*radical jihadi beliefs*" and his backing of the so-called Islamic State. He had also expressed his approval of terrorist attacks, including the October 31 truck attack in New York (BBC News, 2017 (b)).

The second case relates to an incident in the UK northern town of Barrow-in-Furness. A self-confessed far right neo-Nazi, Ethan Stables, was planning to attack the 'New Empire' public house because it was hosting a gay pride event. Stables had set up a neo-Nazi group on Facebook called *"National Socialists Union standing against the New World Order"* and he had invited an entirely innocent woman to join. When he posted his intent to attack the pub on 23 June 2017 on Facebook, horrified at what she saw, she contacted the police who took the threat seriously.

Meantime, the New Empire pub barmaid Katy Bolger was busily getting things ready inside the pub when her world was turned on its head. She said:

> *"Four armed police came in with their guns ready to go. It was so, so frightening. I felt like a deer in the headlights. The first thing they said was 'is there any other way people can get in or out of this pub?' And they said someone had made a terrorist threat - and that this person was going to come in during the event and harm people." - (Casciani, 2018)*

The New Empire had highly-trained and combat-ready doormen: armed police under a duty to secure the location while their colleagues rushed around Barrow in what had become a major manhunt. That same evening, Stables was subsequently arrested and in his apartment police discovered Nazi memorabilia, knives and a small quantity of explosives (Casciani, 2018).

In February 2018, Stables was convicted of planning a terror attack and while the judge had told him to expect a custodial sentence, no pronouncement had been handed down as this book was completed. While the police intervention had been as a result of a tip off, had Stables not posted his intentions on Facebook, he may have successfully executed his planned attack. However, as many police forces the world over know only too well – *"the public are our eyes and ears"*.

6.2 China censors Hong Kong's 'Umbrella Revolution'

There are a number of countries that endeavour to suppress free speech and control the media in an effort prevent the dissemination of what it considers as information that could be potentially compromising to the regime.

In September 2014, I arrived in the semi-autonomous Chinese territory of Hong Kong (HK) just as the largely peaceful Umbrella Revolution protests had started (aka Occupy Central). Beijing would not have wanted news of the protests proliferating across mainland China in case it incited similar unrest and protests in other parts of the country. Consequently, its censors must have gone into overdrive to deal with the traditional news channels and social media postings about these massive pro-democracy street demonstrations in HK. Non-essential travel of Chinese citizens to HK was also restricted by authorities to prevent the spread of first-hand accounts of what was happening in the territory.

The protesters had set up four camps. Three were on Hong Kong island at Causeway Bay, Admiralty and Central, plus a fourth in the Mong Kok District of Kowloon. The camps were all blocking major arterial roads and completely disrupting the traffic flow in these areas, a situation that local authorities surprisingly tolerated for over two months.

While I was in HK, I came across a Shanghai based English teacher who in the interest of anonymity I will refer to as Philip James. Having seen nothing reported about the protests by the mainland China's media, he was surprised when he witnessed the tens of thousands of pro-democracy protesters taking to the streets. He told me that:

> *"Friends in the UK asked me if I had seen the rioting and violence and there were a few Hong Kong media reports of isolated disturbances. But what I have witnessed were peaceful demonstrations by tens of thousands of Hong Kong residents seeking what many of us in the west take for granted - universal suffrage" - (James, 2014)*

What James had observed was exactly what I had observed and which also corresponded with the reports of the civil disobedience campaign published by the HK based Southern China Morning Post.

Chinese Communist Party censors also blocked the website of Britain's national broadcaster, the BBC said in a statement, as tensions rose in Hong Kong between pro-democracy protesters and police. The broadcaster said that the move seemed to be "deliberate censorship". It did not say what may have prompted the move by Beijing, which also blocked the websites of the New York Times, newswire Bloomberg and the BBC's Chinese-language website (Reuters, 2014).

Thinking back to the Orwellian state concept, considering his dependency on the Thought Police in 1984, *Big Brother* would have been largely satisfied with China's central propaganda department's censorship apparatus. Beijing demanded that all China based websites, including its social media platforms, to delete any mention of the unrest.

> *"Spreading the word of unrest over Chinese social networks like Weibo and WeChat became next to*

impossible as messages about the Hong Kong demonstrations were deleted almost as quickly as they were posted" - (Kwong, 2014).

Being semi-autonomous, Hong Kong's internet is currently not subject to censorship like websites and apps in mainland China. Consequently, the free world had total visibility of what was happening there. However, Chinese mainland social media sites such as Weibo do not enjoy that same level of freedom from censorship. Reporting on 29th September 2014, Reuter's correspondent Paul Carsten estimated that on Weibo alone more than 150 posts in every 10,000 had been censored and removed the previous day. This was a record high for 2014, according to censorship watchdog Weiboscope (Carsten, 2014).

Had it been allowed to happen, the proliferation of news concerning events in HK may have caused the protests to spread to other parts of China. Perhaps the Chinese regime was all too conscious of the mass protests of the late 1980's that resulted in the fall of the Berlin Wall along with the collapse of communism in Eastern Europe. In using censorship especially of social media, China largely kept its citizens in the dark about events in Hong Kong and subsequently successfully applied a damage limitation strategy to manage this crisis.

6.3 Social media helps convict hundreds of UK rioters

Following the death of a man shot by police, August 2011 saw rioting break-out in London and quickly spread to several other UK cities. This presented the country not only with a civil emergency but also a threat to both commercial and personal properties. An estimated £200 million of property damage, widespread looting and wanton vandalism occurred along with scores of injuries and five related deaths.

More than 3,000 were ultimately arrested across the country and approximately half were subsequently charged at the very least with causing a disturbance. More than 700 were remanded in custody.

> *"Many of the looters have not bothered to cover their faces as they raided electrical stores, sports shops and off-licences. Some have even posed for a picture afterwards, proudly showing off their haul and posting the images on social-networking sites" - (De Castella & McClatchey, 2011).*

The UK's Regulation of Investigatory Powers Act 2000 regulates public bodies with respect to surveillance and investigation including the interception of communications. The UK police used these powers to insist that Blackberry Messaging and Twitter provided assistance with the identification of the rioters. Writing about the riots in Time, Adams expresses a belief that we are in an age of social media in which disgruntled youth are frequently more skilled with smart phones than are the adults who police them. London authorities believe handheld technologies may have helped those trying to instigate violence to spread their message (Adams, 2011).

The riots were believed to have been made worse by rolling TV news channels and social media such as Twitter and Facebook, according to an independent panel set up by the government to examine the roots of the unrest. However, the expert panel also warned against any knee-jerk plans to shut down social networks in time of public unrest, concluding that "viral silence may have as many dangers as viral noise" - (Halliday, 2011).

> *"Twitter has come under a great deal of criticism for its role in mobilising riots across London, which started in Tottenham, but spread to Enfield, Walthamstow, Waltham Forest, and Brixton over the weekend"* - *(Williams, 2011).*

The sheer volume of arrests necessitated the organisation of emergency court sessions on Sundays. In the UK city of Chester, Jordan Blackshaw and Perry Sutcliffe-Keenan both pleaded guilty to using Facebook in an attempt to fuel riots in the county of Cheshire. They were each jailed for four years although they had pleaded guilty to an offence that carries a maximum sentence of ten years imprisonment. However, lawyers and civil rights groups expressed alarm about what they considered to be 'disproportionate' punishments when compared with other rioters up and down the country (Bowcott, et al., 2011).

Meanwhile, in Manchester, city police initiated a "Shop a Looter" campaign and invited citizens to help identify individuals captured on CCTV. Police also received a deluge of images from members of the public taken using their smart phones. These pictures of suspects were projected on giant digital screens located at two prominent city centre location and were also displayed on mobile advertising vans. The move was part of a wider digital media strategy being deployed by police which also included the use of Twitter, Facebook and Flickr accounts where images of suspects were being displayed (O'Carrol, 2011).

In dealing with this civil disobedience, unlike China's censorship approach to the management of the Umbrella Revolution crisis, ultimately the UK did not resort to suppression of the traditional media or social media. But to reiterate, one of the key factors believed to have incited the riots was the continuous live media streaming of events. However, if at any time the UK Government believes that National Security is threatened then, despite being a democracy rather than a totalitarian regime, it has the power to 'gag' the media by issuing what is known as a 'D-Notice'.

> *"The D-notice system is a peculiarly British arrangement, a sort of not quite public yet not quite secret arrangement between government and media in order to ensure that journalists do not endanger national security" - (Greenslade, 2015).*

Equally like most other nations on the planet, the UK Government also has the means to deny its citizens access to websites that could be located literally anywhere in the world and that would include social media platforms.

6.4 Police use social media metadata to track individuals

Police forces have a massive challenge in monitoring social networks for the prevention and detection of crime due to the sheer volume of material across networks such as Twitter and YouTube. A spokesperson for the Metropolitan Police Service in London explained that the force has made heavy use of social media monitoring tools. Using triangulation to locate and track a cell phone is nothing new. However, with so many individuals seemingly joined at the hip to their smart phones, the 'Met' is capable of tracking them using social media metadata.

> *"Our software can map a person's movements over time, based on the geolocation data attached to their posts, and other pieces of metadata that users may not realise they are beaming out, as it is not always easily accessible to someone just looking at Twitter normally"* - *(Cox, 2016).*

Many social media users post daily updates on their thoughts and feelings or where they are, what they are doing and who they are doing it with. Moreover, they also provide a list of friends and associates that police and security services could find useful. Strange as it may seem, in effect social media has helped to create a society of self-surveillance.

6.5 Witness for the Prosecution and the Defence

What do the UK's Mangetout Grill and Steakhouse restaurant in Southend-on-Sea and the Milton Arms public house in Portsmouth have in common? Like many other hospitality establishments, both have had charity collection boxes stolen from their premises. However, in both these cases, the miscreants were each caught on CCTV. The video footage of their despicable crimes was posted on social media resulting on them being identified, arrested and prosecuted (Millar, 2016) and (Fishwick, 2016).

In Portsmouth, Lee White, 35, was subsequently jailed for 12 weeks after being found guilty of taking three boxes from two pubs and a restaurant (Fishwick, 2016). Following the Mangetout incident, Chelmsford Crown Court was less lenient. Scott Williams, also 35, pleaded guilty to six similar offences and failing to provide a sample for a drugs test and was sentenced to 12 months in prison. In addition, he was ordered to make a £300 contribution to the Royal British Legion charity (Critchell, 2016) and (Noble, 2017).

Many examples of this nature can be found reported on the Internet but Social media is far more powerful than just providing us the means to catch petty criminals. Indeed, it also seems that social media is also being used by 'The Defence' in court cases.

Having worked in the insurance industry myself, albeit on the ICT side of things, I certainly have more than just a passing familiarity with the variety of scams that can often lead to fraudulent claims. One which sticks in my mind for some reason was an incident when a bus encountered black ice and was then involved in a nasty road traffic accident as it collided with a lorry. At the time of the collision there were apparently 17 passengers on the bus. By the time the police and paramedics arrived less than 10 minutes later, the number of potentially injured passengers had mysteriously grown to 28. Today, with so many public transport vehicles fitted with CCTV acts of this nature have become more difficult for individuals to perpetrate.

Elsewhere in the insurance industry, the Florida based Dolman Law Group explains that it used to be very difficult for an attorney to find evidence that could counter someone's claim based on perhaps anxiety or depression. Likewise, it was difficult for an attorney to show that someone was not depressed. Now, with social media, a simple time stamped photo of the plaintiff laughing and drinking with friends will strongly bring into question claims of depression and anxiety. To a jury, it may be hard to believe you're in a state of mental anguish while there is clearly "proof" of you laughing with your friends during a night on the town.

Although the outing may have been a one-time thing—an attempt by your friends to get you out of your funk and you were just playing along—the court and jury may see things differently. Anything posted to social media is considered public domain, in which you have no reasonable expectation of privacy (Dolman Law Group, 2016).

One final thought about this theme of social media being a witness for the prosecution and defence concerns school children and their parents. In the UK there are strict rules governing taking children out of school during term time for the purpose of taking them on holidays. Sometimes the motive is to save money as holiday prices during traditional school holidays are always much higher. Other parents justify it because they may well have a job which is seasonal and demands that they work during the school holiday periods. Head teachers are legally obliged to inform their Local Education Authority (LEA) of both authorised and unauthorised absenteeism.

Each year, there are tens of thousands of reports of parents being fined by their LEA for disregarding these rules. In an attempt to avoid a fine, I also personally know of two of cases where parents phoned the schools to say their children were ill and could not attend and they took the children away on holiday. Their fabricated stories were both compromised by social media. In one case it was a child that posted on Facebook while on holiday and a teacher overheard her friends talking about the post. In the second case, it was one of the parents that checked-in to a posh hotel on Facebook. She presumably forgot that one of her FB friends was on the board of governors of her child's school and who subsequently took exception to the deception. Bad move!!

This is just another example of power of social media imposing a kind of self-policing that I mentioned earlier.

6.6 Is big business now the new Big Brother?

Have you noticed if you click onto an advert on a web page that you are then bombarded by adverts for that product on just about every web page that facilitates sponsored advertising including social media sites? In such cases, what we are experiencing is Artificial Intelligence monitoring our every move while online.

My wife used my computer on one occasion while browsing on a website selling ladies undergarments. Then for what seemed like weeks afterwards I was almost constantly being shown adverts for the various products she had been looking at. I have to say that it didn't look terribly professional when I was using my computer to give a client presentation and a website I needed to visit treated the watching audience to a selection of brassieres. That said, one woman in the audience did raise a laugh at my expense when she enquired *"which one had I decided to purchase?"*

This method of marketing is far from perfect as you can often be shown advertisements for things you may have already purchased. But be warned, every website we visit and our every Internet 'mouse click' is being watched by eyes in the shadows. Meanwhile artificial intelligence algorithms swing into action to exploit the veritable cornucopia of information that we perhaps unwittingly provide!

7 Could social media have made any difference?

While presenting on Crisis Management and Social Media at a seminar recently, a discussion started about two disasters that had both resulted in fatalities – the Piper Alpha oil rig disaster and the 9/11 Twin Towers attack. Whilst the discussion was purely hypothetical, the theme was 'had it been available at a level of service comparable with today, could social media have made any difference to the final death toll'?

In an earlier chapter there were a number of examples where the use of social media had clearly saved lives. In the case of the Piper Alpha oil rig explosion, this occurred around 10 years before the recognised start of the social media era. Conversely, the 9/11 Twin Towers terrorist attack occurred around 4 years after the beginning of the social media age.

Naturally, this is merely conjecture on my part. However, this chapter represents my own personal thoughts on whether or not I believe that the use of social media could have made a difference.

7.1 The Piper Alpha Disaster

> "Around 80 died in the Piper Alpha accommodation block from carbon monoxide poisoning while waiting for direction from management" - (Dakin & Jacobsen, 2014, p. 106)

My book "In Hindsight – a compendium of business continuity case studies" has a sixteen page case study on the Piper Alpha (PA) disaster. This is section includes a brief extract.

Piper Alpha was a large North Sea oil platform operating in the British sector of the North Sea, approximately 120 miles north east of Aberdeen. It was part of a complex network of three rigs that were connected via sub-sea gas or oil pipelines, with PA being utilised as the hub or central platform in the network.

During the night of 6 July 1988 the platform suffered a critical failure that resulted in an explosion. This was followed by an intense gas and oil fuelled fire that very quickly led to the catastrophic loss of the platform.

Prior to the event, there had been a scarcity of training and rehearsals for emergencies and even though training standards had been defined they were not followed. Safety procedures had also been put in place on Piper Alpha but they were largely ignored due to a culture which prioritised targets over safety.

Piper Alpha had several crucial single points of failure, including the positioning of firefighting equipment and lifeboats which severely reduced the chances of saving the rig and its operatives. When the crisis began there was an absence of leadership taking control of the situation. Men died while they waited for their management team to provide direction, if only to instruct them to abandon the rig. With the benefit of hindsight, it is now accepted that the only possible means of survival was in fact to evacuate the rig.

Many of the survivors had no option except to jump into the sea, which for some was from a height of 175 feet (53 m). Some subsequently drowned. Even summer temperatures in the North Sea can be cold enough that the best of swimmers can quickly find themselves in difficulty and heart failure in the prevailing conditions is not unknown.

A total of 167 died that day in 1988 and ever since, Piper Alpha has remained the oil industry's shorthand for *'horror'*. Putting aside any questions marks over connectivity out there in the North Sea, had social media had been available in 1988 it is unlikely that it would have served any useful purpose. Let's remind ourselves that social media in the context of this book is a communications channel for crisis management but, for all intents and purposes, there was no crisis management that day on the oil rig. As covered in section 3.2, if there is no crisis management communications plan then social media will not be of much use in a crisis.

Consequently, I must conclude that many of the operatives caught up in the Piper Alpha disaster were doomed from the outset and, given the prevailing circumstances, there is little or nothing social media could have done to help.

7.2 Terrorism, 9/11 and the Twin Towers

Even though I was yet to reach my teen years, like so many people I can remember exactly where I was when I heard the news of JFK's assassination. It was one of those defining moments in history although at the time I guess the full significance of the event at that young age largely passed me by. Similarly I remember my whereabouts and a sense of sadness when we later lost Martin Luther King, Elvis and John Lennon. However, when it comes to 9/11, emotionally this was on a totally different level. Of course, I wasn't actually there nor did I know any of the victims. But not only do I remember where I was and what I was doing, but even now when I think about what happened, I can still feel the sense of mixed emotions that I experienced back then in 2001. Denial, shock, grief and anger - I'm sure I am not alone.

Eleven years later in 2012, I was awarded a Masters' Degree in Business Continuity, Security and Emergency Management by Bucks New University. My dissertation was entitled 'A Business Response to Terrorism' and as part of my research I looked closely at the events surrounding the 9/11 terrorist attacks. Four aircraft were hijacked that morning by al Qaida terrorists with the intent of crashing them into prestigious high value buildings. However, this study will consider only the two that targeted the Twin Towers of the World Trade Centre in New York.

The attacks occurred approximately 4 years after the generally accepted birth of social media although by September 2001 less than 20 platforms had been launched. Moreover, none matched clientele reach, capability or functionality of platforms like Twitter, Facebook, WhatsApp, or YouTube. In fact it would be another 3.5 years after 9/11 before YouTube was launched yet numerous and often very graphic videos of what happened that day have since been loaded onto the platform.

During my research I came across a number of accounts of what happened that day and not all concurred. In the public domain there are the official findings and reports in addition to a number of conspiracy theories. Many books have since been written – some agree with the official version of events while others do not. For the purposes of this study, rather than speculate on the rights and wrongs of what has been written or said, I will concentrate on the key facts that we know. On the morning of 11ᵗʰ September, 2001:

- American Airlines Flight 11 from Logan Airport, Boston bound for Los Angeles was hijacked and crashed into the North Tower of the World Trade Centre (WTC 1) between floors 93 and 99 at 08:46 am.
- United Airlines Flight 175 from Logan Airport, Boston also bound for Los Angeles was hijacked and crashed into the South Tower of the World Trade Centre (WTC 2) between floors 77 and 85 at 09:03 am.
- WTC 2 collapsed at 09:59 am, fifty-six minutes after the impact of Flight 175.
- WTC 1 collapsed at 10:28 am, one hour and forty-two minutes after the impact of Flight 11.
- A total of 2,996 people are known to have died as a result of the combined terrorist attacks that day and, excluding first responders from the FDNY, PAPD and PDNY, there were 2,152 fatalities recorded as casualties of the Twin Towers attacks. In WTC 1 an estimated 1,500 perished of which 111 were below the point of impact while in WTC 2 the approximate number of fatalities was recorded at 626.
- First responders fatalities were logged as:
  - 343 New York City Fire Department (FDNY) which was the largest loss of life of any emergency response agency in history
  - 37 Port Authority of New York and New Jersey Police Department (PAPD) which was the largest loss of life of any police force in history

- o 23 The Police Department of the City of New York (PDNY) which was the second largest loss of life of any police force in history

Source: (Kean, et al., 2004)

The towers stood at 110 stories each, accommodating a combined workforce of 50,000 and welcoming as many as 200,000 daily visitors. At the time of the attack, estimates of how many people were in the Towers varied from circa 14,000 to 19,000, fortunately well below its full complement. Social media was still very much in its infancy and it would be another 3 years before the arrival of Facebook and 5 years before Twitter's launch.

But let us just remind ourselves of the hypothetical question I referred to in Chapter 7 – *"had it been available at a level of service comparable with today, could social media have made any difference to the final death toll"*.

A great deal of research has been conducted about what happened before, during and after the World Trade Centre attacks. Many lessons have been learned. While reference to other relevant material has been made, this chapter principally considers *'The 9/11 Commission Report'* chaired by Thomas H. Kean plus the results of two surveys that were published following the interviewing of around 400 survivors. They were conducted by:

- The Universities of Greenwich, Ulster and Liverpool – Source: (Glendinning, 2001)
- Center for Disease Control – Source: (CDC, 2004)

The National Institute of Standards and Technology (NIST) reported that immediately before the first aircraft struck WTC 1, there were approximately 8,900 occupants in the Tower and 8,540 in WTC 2. Modelling conducted by the trio of universities estimated that more than 7,500 are likely to have died had the buildings been full at the time of the attack (NB. Federal Investigators put this figure as high as 14,000 : Source - (Choi, 2011)).

It appears that less than 10% of those surveyed actually began to evacuate as soon as the alarm sounded. Some took the time to finish the task they were performing, close down their computers, telephone their families, visit the bathroom and to change their footwear. Some were even reluctant to leave their posts without the express permission of their managers while others delayed their departure as they sought to find out what had happened.

On average, evacuations started approximately 8 to 10 minutes after the alarm although some delayed by as much as 30 minutes. Conversely, there were those individuals who needed no encouragement and left immediately having observed the aircraft crash into the building, smelt aviation fuel or felt the building move from the impact of the crash.

Both WTC 1 and WTC 2 had three primary stairwells designed for emergency egress. Visitors, new employees and temporary staff were at a distinct disadvantage compared with permanent long term occupants. They were less familiar with the building layout not to mention that each floor in WTC 1 and 2 covered an area of approximately one acre. Moreover, they would not have had not had the experience of an evacuation drill. Even so, some 'long termers' admitted getting confused when their designated emergency egress route became unusable due to heavy congestion, fallen rubble, smoke, heat or water on the staircase.

There were those individuals in poor physical shape who found the descent difficult and often slowed down the progress of others. A number of disabled occupants needed assistance and some had to be carried in evacuation chairs. In the case of quadriplegic John Abruzzo whose office was on the 69th floor of WTC 1, it took him and the colleagues who carried him 90 minutes to clear the building, exiting just 10 minutes before it collapsed (Evac Chair, 2001) and (NBC News, 2008).

Criticism was aimed at inappropriate footwear such as high heels and sneakers for also slowing down the exodus. While this may be a justified observation, this does seem a little harsh. Personally I have never seen any Health and Safety manual provide fashion advice on the most appropriate shoes to wear in the event of an emergency evacuation. That said, airlines do instruct passengers to remove high heeled shoes to avoid damaging the emergency escape slides. Finally traffic was by no means one-way with heavily laden firefighters climbing up the stairs to begin fire suppression and rescue.

Were the wrong instructions given to WTC 2 occupants?

> *"The evidence that people were instructed by employers and security guards to remain in the south tower, and thus were condemned to death, is spreading this weekend"* - *(Vulliamy, 2001)*

When the first plane stuck WTC 1, an announcement in WTC 2 urged people to remain at their desks. However, according to 'The 911 Commission report', *"this instruction did not correspond to any prewritten emergency instructions"* (Kean, et al., 2004) . Many people still tried to leave the building only to be turned back by security personnel and Port Authority officials who managed the WTC complex. Anyone sent back to floors that were in the aircraft's impact zone would have had little or no chance of survival, likewise those occupants whose offices were above the point of impact.

In their defence, I think it appropriate to say that the instructions issued by the security personnel and the Port Authority team were based upon what they knew. Let us also remember that 9/11 was unprecedented. Yes, an airplane had hit WTC 1 but it may have just an accident in which case remaining inside WTC 2 may well have been considered to be the safest thing to do. Had they known that there was to be a similar strike on WTC 2 within 20 minutes of WTC 1, the building evacuation would have become critical. Consider what advice is generally given to vulnerable people in the path of a hurricane or tsunami, alternatively those who are in close proximity to a volcano threatening to erupt – **EVACUATE**! But that is because we usually get warning of such events. Moreover, the days of terrorists issuing coded warnings of imminent attacks seem to be behind us.

There is one thing that does puzzle me about whether or not WTC 2 should have been evacuated as soon as WTC 1 was struck by Flight 11, not to mention the other closer buildings in the complex (i.e. WTC 3 and WTC 6 etc.). During my career I have come across a number of life threatening incidents, usually involving a fire or explosion, sometimes both, which have led to Fire and Rescue Services (FRS) insisting that an exclusion zone was established. In fact, there are two such incidents mentioned earlier in this book – the 2007 explosion and fire at Aztec Chemicals in the UK and the 2011 fire at Drop Chemicals in Malta. In both cases the FRS attending set up exclusion zones of 400 metres and 200 metres respectively. Yet WTC 1 was less than 100 metres from WTC 2 and the severity of the incident is utterly beyond comparison with either the Aztec Chemicals or the Drop Chemicals incidents. I had considered whether it was because the local FRS had not arrived on site and yet I came across reports of firefighter Daniel Suhr being killed on the pavement beside WTC 1 just two minutes after the impact of Flight 11 (Dwyer, 2005).

In the following diagram, WTC 3 is on West Street and is almost completely obscured by WTC 1 and WTC 2. The building housed the Marriott World Trade Centre hotel and it suffered collateral damage rendering it beyond repair.

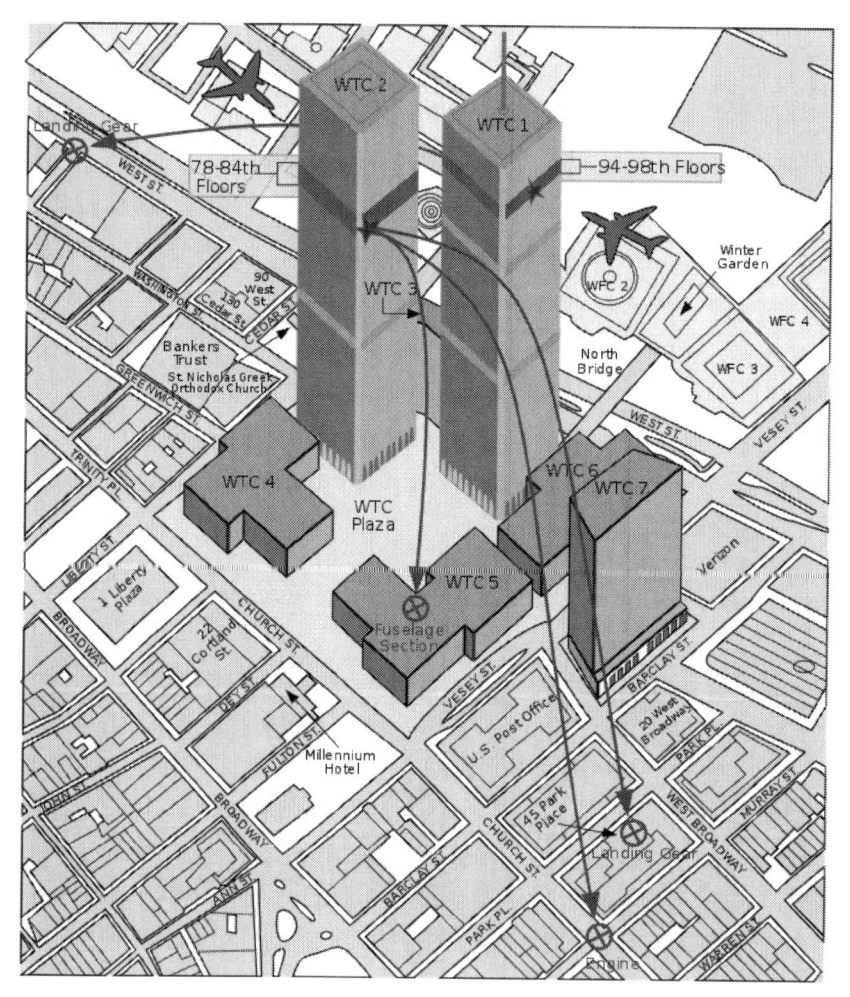

Figure 25: World Trade Centre map – prior to 9/11 attack
Source: MS Word Clipart

147

Communications failed - could Social Media have helped?

The primary building communications systems (e.g. public address system, telephone, elevator telephones etc.) ultimately failed probably due to damage to critical communications hardware. So what if social media websites such as Facebook and Twitter had existed back then in 2001, could it have helped?

> *"Social media would undoubtedly have painted a clearer picture of what happened inside the towers in 2001. Many argue it's an image we don't want to imagine. Vivid, real cries for help and gruesome details of what happens to people in an unimaginably awful situation such as this" - (Praetorius, 2012)*

During the course of my research I have come across a number of sources of information that hypothesise about 9/11 and social media. But they all have one thing in common. In line with the quotation attributed to Dean Praetorius, they all talk solely about outbound communications and what we, on the outside, can learn about what was going on inside. Try as I may, no where can I find any references to how social media may have been able to assist with crisis management communications back in 2001.

We know that social media is a potential communication channel that can be used when there is a crisis. Let's face it, putting aside the various challenges that Mother Nature can throw at the human race, in peacetime crises don't tend to come much bigger than 9/11. So could social media have helped? In my view social media could have been both a help and a hindrance.

7.2.1 The potential benefits from social media

There are a number of inherent benefits of using a social media platform like Twitter as a crisis management communications channel. This hypothesis makes the assumption that Twitter would have been the preferred social media option for the 9/11 crisis management communication plan. First, in addition to having over 500 million members, Twitter will reach people quickly and exponentially. Although it is easy to use and is computer, tablet and smart phone friendly, care needs to be taken vis-à-vis who has access to an organisations Twitter account. It operates in real time and reaction time for a Tweet can be instantaneous.

Sadly we must accept that social media could not have helped the occupants in WTC 1 trapped above the impact zone. With the decision not to attempt a roof top rescue, there was no possibility of them escaping since the three emergency egress staircases had been destroyed. What is more, it was standard practice for the doors to the roof remained locked for security reasons. When a 'lock release' order was finally issued at 9:30, damage to the software controlling the system meant the order could not be executed. However, I can see some situations where the presence of social media may have helped other occupants of both WTC 1 and WTC 2. For example:

- With the communications system failures, social media could have enabled occupants to keep in touch with WTC site management and emergency services. While many could have used cell phones they would only have provided a one-to-one communication channel rather than the ubiquitous reach that social media would provide.

- In addition to keeping WTC 1 and WTC 2 occupants informed, occupants of the other WTC buildings could have been updated from a single point of control
- Social media could have been used to direct people away from perhaps an impassable egress and redirect them to another more suitable means of escape
- Although many trapped Twin Tower occupants used their cells phones to speak to loved ones, leave them voicemails or send them text messages, the availability of social media may well have enabled occupants to have better connected with loved ones in those final minutes.
- Kept the local population advised on the direction of the smoke plume and especially as we now know that a tremendous amount of toxic dust was generated by the incident
- In WTC 2, Stairwell "A" was still intact after the impact and a small number of people actually managed to escape from the vicinity of the impact zone. Brian Clark, Ron Di Francesco and Richard Fern from Euro Brokers on the 84th floor and Stanley Praimnath from Fuji Bank on the 81st floor in WTC 2 all made it out of the building via Stairwell "A" (Koler, 2011) and (Hobson, 2016). However, the vast majority of those above the impact zone opted to head for the roof unaware that a rescue by helicopter had already been ruled out by emergency services due to the thick smoke. Had social media been available, maybe some of

these individuals could have been redirected towards this potential escape route.

- Following the collapse of WTC 2, at 10:00 am all firefighters were instructed via radio to withdraw from WTC 1 although numerous individuals did not receive the transmission. Some subsequently received the message by word of mouth from colleagues; others never received the message at all. In crisis management we need to ensure that when one communication channel fails, predetermined alternatives have been identified. In this instance, social media could have provided a multitude of messaging streams. However, the originator of the radio message would not necessarily have known who had and who had not heard the original radio instruction to withdraw unless each firefighter was asked to respond and confirm.

7.2.2 The negative aspects of using social media

In the previous section we considered the benefits of using Twitter as a primary communication channel for the 9/11 crisis management. As we continue to hypothesise, we must remember that social media is not a panacea and it would certainly have had its downsides. That said, by adopting Twitter, some would point to being restricted to 140 characters per Tweet as being a disadvantage. However, I believe that time is of the essence and messages should be kept short and to the point – avoid monologues or chunky communications. You are using valuable time in writing them and recipients having to read them. So let's consider social media's potential shortcomings:

- If we first consider the WTC 2 PA system announcement instructing people to return to their desks when WTC 1 was struck, had that same message been tweeted it would have presumably had the same affect. In retrospect we now know that advice was wrong and evacuation of WTC 2 should have commenced immediately Flight 11 crashed into WTC 1.
- Twitter is an open social media platform. As such anything put out on Twitter would be in the public domain. Using it is comparable to having a conversation in a very public place. With such a high profile crisis as 9/11 this is bound to generate a lot of chatter or tweeting from people who have nothing to do with the WTC in fact they could be located almost anywhere on the planet and still be able to join the conversations. This would necessitate WTC occupants having to *"separate the wheat from the chaff"* – in other words they would need to ignore much of the irrelevant chatter and look for pertinent messages presumably from the emergency services or the WTC site management team. In the case of 9/11, the consequences could be valuable time is lost that should have been used to enable the Twin Tower occupants to successfully escape.
- Another downside of social media is its ability to facilitate the rapid spread of rumours and misinformation. Governments and organisations alike are finding themselves grappling with the misinformation that social networking often spawns. For example, after the 2015 terrorist attacks in Paris, approximately 10.7 million tweets were posted in a 24 hour period. Remember Twitter is of course just one of many social media platforms. Much of

this Paris focused information was incorrect or arguably *'economical with the truth'* (Whitten, 2015). Moreover, in a fast moving incident like 9/11 moderating the volume of comments posted on social media is just not going to happen.

- We saw in section 4.3 how the al Shabaab terrorist had made full use of Twitter to provide a running commentary of their attack on the Westgate shopping mall in Kenya. Had the 9/11 terrorist also had access to social media they could have conducted a campaign of misinformation that could have further confused the situation for people both inside and outside of the Twin Towers.

- The last point I wanted to raise in this section was with regard to what is being referred to as *"inattentional blindness"* syndrome, also known as perceptual blindness. This is a psychological lack of attention that is not in any way associated with any vision defects or deficits and I have personally discovered that this is widespread in places such as Hong Kong. I will talk more about that in that in the next chapter. However, in brief it means people walking around with their eyes firmly fixed on their smartphones totally oblivious to everyone and everything around them. They often walk into solid objects such as a wall and I have personally experienced them walking into me. Imagine a situation like 9/11 where the occupants of the towers are trying to evacuate but are obstructed by others insisting on concentrating on their smartphones in case they miss an important message. We have already seen a number of things earlier in this chapter that slowed down the evacuation – social media could have been just one more thing to do the same and it could have cost more lives.

In working through this hypothesis, had a social media been available on that fateful day in 2001 with a capability comparable with its 2018 equivalent, I can see both positive and negative aspects of it being used as a means of crisis communications. My key conclusions are as follows:

1. Those unfortunate individuals who were above the impact zone in the WTC 1 had no chance of escape regardless of whether social media had been available or not. Rescue from the roof by helicopter had been ruled out not to mention that the doors to the roof were locked and could not be released. To compound their fate, their three emergency egress routes had also been destroyed.

2. Excluding first responders, it is believed that there were more than one hundred individuals who were below the impact line in WTC 1 but did not manage to evacuate before the building collapsed. They had had one hour and forty two minutes to make good their escape. It can only be assumed that they were prevented from escaping perhaps because they were trapped, injured, disabled or they were assisting someone else to evacuate and simply ran out of time. I consider it unlikely that social media could have been of much benefit for them except to emphasise the heightened severity of the situation after WTC 2 had collapsed.

3. Despite the potential disruption to the evacuation of WTC 2 that could have been caused by inattentional blindness mentioned earlier in this chapter, I see one possible

situation where civilian lives could have been saved by social media. We know that a small group in WTC 2 located above the impact zone actually made it out via stairwell 'A' while others made the fatal decision to ascend to the roof and wait to be rescued from there. Had social media been used to advise people in WTC 2 that one of the emergency egress routes was still open, and that there would be no rooftop rescue attempt, just maybe more people could have made good their escape from the tower before it collapsed. The downside of the 'no rooftop rescue' announcement would be to also have told those trapped in WTC 1 that their predicament was hopeless.

I hope my theoretical perspective on the pros and cons of social media being used during the 9/11 crisis actually makes sense. But as I stressed at the outset, it is only my opinion and I would appreciate hearing your comments too.

8 On a more personal note......

In my view, despite how it may appear, all is not sweetness and light for the end user in the land of social media. Even if most users don't appreciate it yet, as well as the previously discussed darker side of social media such as cyber bullying, grooming, sexting and trolling, it definitely has other downsides as the following sections endeavour to highlight.

But I recently witnessed something leaving me unsure whether to laugh or cry. My twenty something year old niece was reading the cooking instructions on the back of the box of a ready-meal she had purchased. Then clearly without thinking, she instinctively started to try and scroll down the information as though she was reading the instructions on a smart phone or tablet. When the error of her ways was pointed put to her, she laughed it off and admitted that this was not the first time she had done something like that. Apparently, she had also tried to do the same thing while reading a paperback presumably thinking she was reading her Kindle.

8.1 Can social media damage your health?

I have made several business trips to Hong Kong (HK) in recent years where I have usually stayed in the Causeway Bay area. HK has an amazing Mass Transit Railway (MTR) that carries close to 5 million passengers every day. While travelling on this MTR you cannot help but notice that the vast majority of standing passengers position themselves sideways on to the direction the train is heading. Moreover, not many will be holding-on to any grab rails or poles because, having mastered the art of maintaining their balance in a moving train, both hands are seemingly permanently attached to their smart phones as they access their preferred social media apps. I also noticed on a recent visit to China that this technique had been embraced on the MTR in the city of Xian, home of the Terracotta Warriors.

"Beware the smart phone zombies blindly wandering around Hong Kong........'Distracted walking', as the experts call it, is a growing annoyance in the MTR and malls and on the streets of Hong Kong" - *(Sharp, 2015)*

But back in HK, the nearest MTR station to my usual hotel is Tin Hau and to reach it I have to use a pedestrian crossing spanning a busy dual carriageway. While waiting for the 'Green' light to proceed substantial crowds can build up on both sides. Many of these pedestrians will have their heads down with eyes firmly fixed on their smart phone screens. When the two crowds get the 'Green' light, they move towards each other and invariably meet on the central reservation where chaos can ensue as they collide. This practice has even spawned a Cantonese colloquialism - *dai tau juk*, or head-down tribe. Being considerably larger than your average HK resident, I have occasionally had locals walking into me and bouncing off while their smart phones take their chances as they bounce off the road. Following the lead set by Chongqing in mainland China, in some areas of Hong Kong, pavements have been partitioned and now have designated mobile phone lanes in an attempt to alleviate the frustration that non-phone users experience.

Of course, walking and texting is nothing new. YouTube carries many excellent and often amusing examples of people with their heads down walking into walls or lampposts, falling downstairs or into water. Some even stepping into busy roads without looking first. Chief Thomas Ripoli from the Fort Lee New Jersey Police Department told CNN that he was cracking down on jaywalking because of the rise in social media related accidents (CNN News, 2017). Injuries resulting from such acts could also invalidate insurance claims as insurance companies could point to negligence resulting in self-inflicted injuries. Scientists are now referring to this phenomenon as "inattentional blindness". Another classic example caught on CCTV shows a man on a scooter fiddling with his smart phone only to drive into a sink hole which had opened up in front of him a shortly before he plunged in. Fortunately, he escaped without injury.

Even more concerning is the rise in road traffic accidents caused by vehicle drivers not just texting but using social media while driving. In the UK there have been a number of prosecutions and in one instance a lorry driver was handed down a ten year prison sentence for killing four people while using his smart phone on a major road. Returning momentarily to Hong Kong, mobile phone use is now recognised as the leading cause of death behind the wheel, a point brilliantly reinforced by a very effective short film entitled "MCL cinema Hong Kong Mobile phone car crash advertising effective".

History has taught us that smoking can cause heart and lung disease, excessive drinking damages the liver while taking recreational drugs can result in mental health problems. So what about social media ? Having made a point of observing the social media addicts of today, using their smart phones, especially the millennials, it also makes me wonder if they are sowing the seeds that will result in repetitive strain injury (RSI) later in life. OK, so unlike cancer, heart disease or liver failure, RSI is not life threatening. However, a doctor in Granada is advising fellow physicians to be "mindful" of the injuries that can result from using instant messaging services, after she diagnosed a 34-year-old pregnant woman with she referred to as "*WhatsAppitis*". Such was the profile and import of the case in medical circles that it was featured in the medical journal 'The Lancet'. This explained that the patient was suffering sudden pain in both wrists after waking up in the morning (Kassam, 2014).

Unfortunately, it seems the threat to health from social media goes well beyond just RSI. A poll of around fifteen-hundred 14 to 24-year-olds shows Instagram, Facebook, Snapchat and Twitter increased feelings of inadequacy and anxiety. Four of the five most popular forms of social media harm young people's mental health according to research by two health organisations. Clearly more research will need to be done at the very least to understand the potential links between heavy social media usage and reports of growing sleep problems, feelings of anxiety, depression and loneliness.

> "The findings follow growing concern among politicians, health bodies, doctors, charities and parents about young people suffering harm as a result of sexting, cyberbullying and social media reinforcing feelings of self-loathing and even the risk of them committing suicide" - (Campbell, 2017)

All things considered, perhaps social media platforms should carry a mandatory health warning !

8.2 Emotions to the fore

"Anger is the emotion that spreads the most easily over social media" - Teddy Wayne, New York Times, 2013

The mantra of an old manager of mine was *"if it's not in writing it didn't happen or it was never said"*. He would insist that minutes of meetings were properly recorded as well as encouraging us all to formally communicate in writing. Now I remember the days when to communicate in writing with someone in the office you used pen and paper. So if you received a memo or letter that was shall we say *'provocative'*, in the time it took to write a response, you usually would have the opportunity to cool off.

Then Email came along in the late 70's and that cooling off period just evaporated overnight. There was a tendency for people to react immediately and shoot off a response before they had had time to reflect and perhaps react with a more measured response.

Social media takes that instant response to another level entirely. You can for example sit in a restaurant reach for you smart phone and put a derogatory comment on TripAdvisor about the service or the meal you've had before you've even been presented with the bill. One wonders how many people choose to take this route rather than raise the issue with a member of staff and give them a chance to address the issue there and then.

On the other side of the coin, organisations should be continually monitoring social media for comments about their brand, services, products and employees. Moreover, be prepared to respond quickly to any negative postings. If you feel the comments are unjustified then be ready to say so and state your case.

8.3 Social media can inhibit your career

Back in the day, long before social media had appeared on the scene, one former employer of mine ensured that we employees were made well aware of certain "Do's" and "Don'ts" which looking back I don't think were unreasonable. First the most likely reasons (although I am sure there were others) that would get you fired were if you were caught stealing from the company or if you hit a fellow employee. We were also told that what we did in our private lives was our own affair providing that it did not inhibit us from doing our jobs or in some way brought the company into disrepute. I would imagine that spending time on personal social media activity during working hours has since been added to the list of sins that one could commit. At the very least it could probably invite a 'team talk' from your manager and possibly a mention in your next annual appraisal.

In previous sections, there have been cases of people being fired because their social media activity had constituted what can only be seen as an insider threat to their employer. Whether they were using their employer's social media accounts or their own personal accounts seems largely irrelevant and it harks back to my previous employer's warning regarding bringing the company into disrepute. In each instance their actions had threatened to harm their employer's brand and reputation and their respective management had some serious damage limitation activity to perform.

Now this brings me to the point of what in the UK we call 'throwing a sickie'. That is to say that you phone your employer and tell them you are not coming into work as you are ill when in fact you are perfectly healthy. Providing the nature of the fictitious illness is plausible, most people will generally get away with taking the odd day off in this way. In 1982, I was living in the small UK town of Petersfield which I guess at the time would have had a population of between 12,000 and 13,000. Probably very few people in the UK would have heard of Petersfield let alone known where it was. That all changed on 2nd January when the name of Petersfield was well and truly put on the map. England was playing rugby at Twickenham against Australia when one very large breasted young lady called Erica Roe ran topless onto the pitch. She was subsequently apprehended and arrested by police but news of the event caught the attention and imagination of both national television channels and newspapers. Erica became front page news and gained instant fame with articles frequently mentioning that she worked at the Petersfield Bookshop. However, her employer was probably not impressed by Erica's new found celebrity status. Not only had she arguably brought her employer into disrepute but she had phoned in sick that morning. The story that was circulating in Petersfield was that Erica had been fired but then quickly reinstated when the gentle flow of customers into the Bookshop grew into a torrent with people coming from far and wide wanting to meet Erica. Thanks to her antics at the rugby match, Erica had inadvertently raised the profile of the Bookshop and substantially boosted sales.

So why am I telling you about Erica Roe? Well, by streaking at Twickenham, she got herself well and truly noticed and completely compromised her story about being sick. Back in 1982, shooting yourself in the foot in this way wasn't so easy to achieve. But today, with social media, it is simplicity personified and so many people inadvertently do it without realising until it is too late. They phone in sick and then do something daft like put a post on social media perhaps checking-in somewhere or posting a timestamped photo showing themselves eating in a restaurant or drinking with friends. If these little faux-pas somehow come to the attention of one's boss, rest assured that this kind of careless action can turn into a career inhibiting move.

But there is another way that social media can harm our careers.

> *"More than 90% of recruiters and hiring managers have visited a potential candidate's profile on a social network as part of the screening process. And a whopping 69% of recruiters have rejected a candidate based on content found on his or her social networking profiles"* - (Swallow, 2017)

Now some people take issue with prospective employers and recruitment agencies making judgements on potential candidates' based upon their social media entries believing it is an invasion of privacy. While you might feel strongly that it is an unethical practice, at the time of writing, it certainly isn't illegal. Equally, providing it does not contravene the law nor breach any of the social media platforms' T's & C's, I believe that every individual has the right to post whatever pictures of themselves that they like. That said, I have had the dubious pleasure of having seen photographs on Facebook of individuals in a drunken / compromising state or dropping their pants to reveal their buttocks or 'mooning' as it is sometimes called. However, probably the most distasteful example I came across was someone using their tongue in an apparent attempt to perform a tonsillectomy on their partner.

Call me old fashioned but these individuals must remember that those posts and images are likely to end up in the public domain and may one day come back to haunt them. So too could derogatory remarks about your old boss, your colleagues or perhaps a client. Recruiters may well believe that your social media posts are a depiction of you and your character and that is why employers could well use it against you.

Liz Ryan, *CEO / founder of Human Workplace and author of Reinvention Roadmap*, published the following tips on the Forbes website about cleaning up your social media presence. She lists five social media mistakes that could really slow down your job search:

- Risqué or racy content on your social media pages
- Offensive sentiments or images on your profile and/or extreme political or religious views
- Photos or discussion about illegal activities (even if in a joking manner)
- Images and updates that reference a focus on partying and getting crazy
- Angry or argumentative comments and threads

Source: (Ryan, 2017)

But has the warning light already come on? A survey by cyber-security firm Norton and recruitment firm Reed says UK millennials (18 - 34 year-olds) are now concerned how their social media activity might interfere, and damage, their professional careers - (Fadilpašić, 2015).

For a five year period during my career I managed a pool of up to 1,500 consultants across five countries. In my time I have read thousands of Curriculum Vitae's (resumes), long since lost count of the number of interviews I have performed and employed hundreds of successful candidates. But let's face it, a CV's content may be a work of fiction, the candidate may be economical with the truth at interviews and references can be concocted. So I must admit that had social media been around I would have certainly used it and most definitely thought twice about employing someone whose presence on social media was, shall we say, arguably unsavoury.

More recently, I was asked for my opinion of a candidate that one of my clients was considering employing. On that occasion I was able compare her LinkedIn profile, which in effect was her professional shop window, with her CV and discovered that there was certainly a rather glaring disparity. As an interview had already been arranged, the interviewer asked her to explain the discrepancies. She simply couldn't! On reflection, if you analysed everything she claimed to have done in her CV, she was probably over 100 years old!

"If the information is in the public domain, an employer would be dumb not to look at it. Just good due diligence!"
– Andrew Hunter Johnston, CCLA, 2017

If you feel you may be vulnerable in this respect, periodically, run a Google search on yourself to ascertain what your current or prospective employers' might get to see. In the event that you come across something potentially compromising, endeavour to trace the origin of the entry and, assuming it's not you, approach the individual who posted it and request they delete it. If the source proves elusive or reluctant to take down the content, Google or the administrators of the specific website(s) you are concerned with may be prepared to help.

9 Conclusion

Through the pages of this book, we have seen in all its various forms the multifaceted phenomenon that we have come to know as social media. The variety of case studies has demonstrated that it can be a force for good as well as a force for evil. Ever since the launch of its first platform, "Six Degrees", in 1997, for many it has become an essential part of their lives whether on a personal or a professional basis. There are those often referred to as millennials for who social media looks to have become an addiction. Many appear to have allowed it to effectively take control of their lives as they keep themselves available day and night ready to respond to its every beck and call.

Social media provides us with a constant stream of information from just about every source imaginable including the authorities, news portals, friends and family, businesses and so on. It allows us to reach out to like-minded people around the world. But social media does not arbitrate whether the information it has a penchant for bombarding us with is genuine or false. Consequently, we have experienced how it can lie to us but then again, who coined the expression *"don't shoot the messenger"*?

> *"America is the land of forgiveness. We've forgiven Mike Tyson, Bill Clinton, Exxon, Tylenol, and a rogue's gallery of corporate and individual miscreants and near do wells. You'll be forgiven too, if you say you're sorry and mean it"* - (Baer, 2012)

We have seen organisations guilty of misdemeanours offered up by social media as the proverbial sacrificial lamb only for us to show forgiveness and clemency. Perhaps the best example in this book is United Airlines that was certainly guilty of two major high profile faux-pas and yet it saw its sales, profits and stock market value soar. At the other end of the corporate scale, the husband and wife owned American diner 'Mustard' was slated on TripAdvisor as, because of its popularity, it was full and had no vacant tables one evening. Yet loyal customers took to Facebook in their droves to express their unequivocal support for the restaurant, its food and its staff. Despite the unmistakeable disparity between the size and worth of these two organisations, perhaps in their own way United Airlines and Mustard have provided evidence that supports the argument that *there is no such thing as bad publicity*.

I have come across people who have expressed concern about social media making mistakes. I'm sorry – I beg to differ! Social media does not make mistakes – that's the human element of the equation and examples of what I would call *'finger trouble'* were articulated in Chapter 4. However, what social media does have is a very big metaphorical mouth and it can be incredible indiscrete while it will indiscriminately tell the world about your mistakes! But this can also work against those organisations that are victims and have fallen prey to an insider threat. By using social media as their *'weapon of choice'*, the potential for damaging their employer's brand and reputation is enormous.

We have seen that all is not sweetness and light in the social media domain. While it can clearly be an asset to crisis management communications, it can also be instrumental in causing the crisis in the first place. But its darker side is potentially far worse. It has provided a new and far more efficient platform for those individuals who choose to engage in the abhorrent practices of cyber bulling, sexting, trolling and grooming. Moreover, there is evidence of terrorists providing live commentaries of their heinous actions through Twitter while glorifying their militants' deeds. And yet, it can't be all bad as social media can and has saved lives too!

Social media influenced disruption in the classroom is massive and yet there is the potential and opportunity there for it to be harnessed as a core subject. We should all remember that a crisis does not necessarily have to be business related – it can be of a personal nature too. We have learned that it presents a threat to both our physical and psychological wellbeing. It can also affect our personal standing especially in the eyes of our employers – both present and future. Moreover, as some criminals have discovered, social media can be seen acting for the prosecution as well as the defence.

My penultimate conclusion is a message for those individuals who have an aversion to the concept of living within a 'Big Brother' state. *Sorry, things just got worse as social media has provided Big Brother with another means of watching you.* Just remember that if you really don't want the world at large to see your photos or read your social media posts, regardless of whatever security settings you may have selected, simply don't post them onto social media in the first place.

In 2018, social media reached the 21st anniversary of its original launch yet without the Internet it would not exist. What many people don't appreciate is that the Internet has been around since the late 1960's although it wasn't known by that name during its early years. I certainly believe that it would have been seen as having the potential to dynamically influence the evolution of information technology. But there is little evidence to suggest that anyone gave much consideration for the need for some form of effective security. Now in the 21st century the daily threat that both individuals and organisations face from cyberspace is the consequential legacy. Simplistically, I liken it to a building that has been constructed to the owner's specification. Then retrospectively the owner decides that he wants a lift installed too. To add a lift to a finished building is far more difficult and costly than if you had included it in the original design. I feel a parallel of the lift scenario exists with security and the Internet.

I can also see a similarity between the evolution of the Internet and social media. When companies started developing their respective social media platforms they would have undoubtedly focused on the unique and positive selling points of their products. Yet, as we have seen in this book, despite the benefits it offers, there is a great deal of negativity surrounding social media much of which is completely unacceptable to society at large. To adopt a human analogy, while often appearing as a well-meaning individual, social media is not particularly fussy about the company it keeps. It is known to occasionally mix with undesirable elements such as criminals and terrorists. With its 21st birthday upon us, social media may have come of age yet sadly there are instances when it still behaves like a juvenile delinquent.

10 Do you want to become a best-selling author

Have you ever dreamed about publishing your own book but for one reason or another it has never actually happened.

My book "In Hindsight" got to Number One on the Amazon best sellers lists. Perhaps I can help you to achieve your dream too.

To find out more without any obligation please visit our website at:

http://www.bcm-consultancy.com/publish-my-book

11 Review Request

Thank you for reading this book which I hope you have not only enjoyed but also found to be useful. I would very grateful if you would post an honest review as your support really does matter and it genuinely does make a difference. I do read the reviews and I will study your feedback and make any appropriate changes.

If you would like to leave a review then all you need to do is go to the review section on the book's Amazon page. You will see a big button that says "Write a customer review" – just click on it and you are good to go.

However, a brief note if I may to **American readers**. Being British I naturally wrote the book using the Queen's English so I apologise if you came across words that were not spelt the way you would expect of an American publication (e.g. centre / center, specialise / specialize etc.). As Winston Churchill once said *'we are divided by a common language'*.

Many thanks for your support which is very much appreciated.

Best wishes

Robert Clark

Website :	www.bcm-consultancy.com
Email :	Robert.clark@bcm-consultancy.com
Linked-In :	mt.linkedin.com/in/maltabusinesscontinuity/
Twitter :	@BCMConsultancy

12 Other Books by the Author

These books are available in both Kindle and paperback format.

"I wanted to send you a note of congratulations on your book, which I've just had the pleasure of reading. I think it is a very useful contribution to available literature and hopefully will lead to an appreciation of why BCM is essential"

Dr Kevin Pollock MBCI

"I wish I'd had a copy of this book when I started out in Business Continuity. All in all, an easy read. This book certainly deserves the 'must read' tagline and should form part of the essential library of anyone involved in the validation of Business Continuity Plans"

Mark Fenech MBA MBCI MIRM

"*This informative book is written in an easy going and conversational manner, but the message it brings to the table is critical to understanding the meaning of any forthcoming pandemic threat and considerations of how to mitigate the effects, where possible, to you and your organisation*"

Owen Gregory MSc BA MBCI MBCS

The books are all available on Amazon in both Kindle and paperback format.

13 Glossary of Terms

AKA	Abbreviation for 'also known as'
Arab Spring	The series of protests and demonstrations across the Middle East and North Africa that commenced in 2010, became known as the "**Arab Spring**",
BBC	British Broadcasting Corporation
BoA	Bank of Albuquerque
Brexit	Short hand for Britain existing the European Union
Broad Church	A wide range of different examples
BS 11200:2014	British Standard for crisis management which was introduced in 2014 and replaced PAS 200.
BuzzFeed	BuzzFeed is an independent digital media company delivering news and entertainment to hundreds of millions of people globally
Catalytic terrorism	An act of terrorism committed in full view of the media
CCTV	Close Circuit Television
CEO	Chief Executive Officer
CFO	Chief Financial Officer
Champions League	This is an annual continental club football competition organised by the Union of European Football Associations and contested by top-division European clubs
CIO	Chief Information Officer
CNN	Cable Network News

CPD	Civil Protection Department – Fire and Rescue Services in the Republic of Malta
C-Suite	The expression C-Suite is derived from the titles of top senior executives which tend to start with the letter C, for chief, as in chief executive officer (CEO), chief financial officer (CFO), chief information officer (CIO), and chief technical officer (CTO).
Deepwater Horizon	The Deepwater Horizon was the oil rig operated by BP and was at the centre of the massive oil spill in Gulf of Mexico in 2010.
Ebola	Ebola is highly contagious and potentially fatal haemorrhagic fever that killed over 11,000 in West Africa between 2013 and 2014.
FAQ's	Frequently asked questions
Faux-pas	Derived from the French language meaning 'a mistake'.
FEMA	Federal Emergency Management Agency
Foot and Mouth	An infectious and sometimes fatal viral disease that affects cloven-hoofed animals. Usually treated by destroying all cattle in the infected herd plus strict quarantine measures. Human variant is known as Creutzfeldt–Jakob disease
GPS	Global Positioning Satellite
Hashtag	A hashtag is a type of metadata tag used on social networks such as Twitter and other microblogging services
Inattentional blindness	Inattentional blindness, also known as perceptual blindness, is a psychological lack of attention that is not

	associated with any vision defects or deficits. Individuals who walk with their eyes firmly fixed on the smart phones while totally oblivious to everyone and everything around them are said to suffer from the condition.
Intifada	An Arab word with a literal meaning of shaking off by means of an uprising.
Juvenile delinquent	A young person often a minor who habitually commits criminal acts
Kawasaki disease	A rare childhood disease that affects the blood vessels. In extreme cases it can be fatal.
Machupo virus	Also known as Bolivian haemorrhagic fever that can also generate neurological symptoms. It can be fatal in around 10% of cases.
Manchester city centre exclusion zone	In 1996 the city centre of Manchester in the UK was the target of terrorists who detonated the biggest peacetime bomb experienced in the UK. Emergency services declared an exclusion prohibiting entry of non-authorised individuals due to the extensive structural damage caused by the explosion. The exclusion zone was in place for several months during which tine around 200 businesses went bankrupt..
Mea culpa	This is a Latin phrase which is an admission of blame – 'my fault'
Mega terrorism	An act of terrorism that has an objective to maximise human casualties
MTR	Mass Transit Railway (e.g. subway trains etc.)
N^3	Next News Network
NBC	National Broadcasting Company

NGO	Non-Governmental Organisation which would be a non-profit organization operating independently of any government
NSPCC	National Society for the Prevention of Cruelty to Children – a UK charity
Occupy Central	Aka The Umbrella Revolution was a series of peaceful pro-democracy demonstrations in Hong Kong.
Off-Licence	Liquor store
Orwellian	Based on the book 1984 by George Orwell, an Orwellian society is dystopian and will often be associated with the expression 'Big Brother is watching'
PA system	Public address communication system
Paris Accord	The name given to the 2015 international climate change agreement so called as it was signed in Paris
PAS 200	The publically available specification (PAS) was the standard for Crisis Management prior to being replaced by BS 11200 in 2014
Repetitive Strain Injury (RSI)	This can be a painful condition that manifests itself in muscles, tendons and nerves and can be caused by repetitive movements (e.g. typing etc.) over a long period of time.
Risk Register	A list of risks that an organisation or a country has assessed and identified as presenting a threat.
Sahelian Drought	The Sahel area of Africa sits below the Sahara desert and stretches from the Atlantic in the west to the Indian Ocean in the east. The Sahelian drought was first recorded in the 17th century and can last for several decades.

Savitch's three goal model	Savitch identified three conditions that terrorist usually seek to achieve when perpetrating an attack. They are Smart, Catalytic and Mega terrorism. Please refer to mega terrorism, smart terrorism and catalytic terrorism for more information.
Severe Acute Respiratory Syndrome (SARS)	SARS is a respiratory disease that first emerged in 2002 in the Chinese province of Guangdong. It was a novel virus and spread quickly to 26 countries and can be fatal.
Sexting	This is the sending or receiving of sexually explicit messages and / or images
Smart Terrorism	An act of terrorism that is looking to maximise critical asset damage
SME's	Small and Medium size Enterprises
Spanish Influenza	This influenza was first diagnosed in 1918 and evolved into a global pandemic resulting in circa 50 million casualties worldwide.
Spectrum 128 +3 computer	This was an early personal computer manufactured by Amstrad and released in the UK in 1987. It came with 128KB RAM and a floppy disk drive.
Stakeholder	An individual who has an interest or a concern in an organisation
The Lancet	First published in 1873, the Lancet is a weekly general medical journal. It is one of the world's oldest and best known general medical journals
The WHO	The World Health Organisation
Thought Police	This was the secret police as portrayed in George Orwell's novel 1984.

Troll / Trolling	A troll is someone who uses the Internet to promote discord by posting inflammatory and usually false remarks about third parties.
UK	United Kingdom
UK NRR	United Kingdom's National Risk Register
Umbrella Revolution	See occupy central
Vis-à-vis	Derived from the French language and meaning 'with regard to'
Weiboscope	This is a project at the Journalism and Media Studies Centre at the University of Hong Kong which tracks and produces annual and quarterly reports on the most important censored Weibo posts of the year.

14 Works Cited

Adams, W. L., 2011. *Were Twitter or BlackBerrys Used to Fan Flames of London's Riots?.* [Online]
Available at:
http://content.time.com/time/world/article/0,8599,2087337,00.html
[Accessed 23 12 2017].

Agnes, M., 2017. *HOw to get your crisis communications right first time.* [Online]
Available at: https://youtu.be/Rat5C2FcHSg
[Accessed 31 12 2017].

Agnes, M., 2017. *United Airlines, What Were You Thinking?.* [Online]
Available at: https://melissaagnes.com/united-airlines-thinking/
[Accessed 31 12 2017].

Alexander, H., 2013. *Tweeting terrorism: How al Shabaab live blogged the Nairobi attacks.* [Online]
Available at:
http://www.telegraph.co.uk/news/worldnews/africaandindianocean/keny
a/10326863/Tweeting-terrorism-How-al-Shabaab-live-blogged-the-
Nairobi-attacks.html
[Accessed 12 12 2017].

Arthur, C., 2013. *Burger King's woes continue after Twitter account gets hacked.* [Online]
Available at:
https://www.theguardian.com/technology/2013/feb/18/burger-king-
twitter-account-hack
[Accessed 02 01 2018].

Ashford, W., 2013. *Social media a security challenge and opportunity.* [Online]
Available at: http://www.computerweekly.com/feature/Social-media-a-

security-challenge-and-opportunity
[Accessed 02 02 2018].

Averill, J. et al., 2005. *Federal Investigation of the Evacuation of the World Trade Center on September 11. 2001.* [Online]
Available at: http://fire.nist.gov/bfrlpubs/fire07/PDF/f07018.pdf
[Accessed 05 12 2017].

Baer, J., 2012. *Don't Be Scared, Be Prepared – How to Manage a Social Media Crisis.* [Online]
Available at: http://www.convinceandconvert.com/social-media-strategy/dont-be-scared-be-prepared-how-to-manage-a-social-media-crisis/
[Accessed 04 02 2018].

BBC - On This Day, 2008. *1996: 'The whole city shook'.* [Online]
Available at:
http://news.bbc.co.uk/onthisday/hi/witness/june/15/newsid_2963000/2963780.stm
[Accessed 22 01 2012].

BBC - US & Canada News, 2018. *Florida shooting: At least 17 dead in high school attack.* [Online]
Available at: http://www.bbc.co.uk/news/world-us-canada-43066226
[Accessed 14 02 2018].

BBC - US & Canada News, 2018. *Russia-Trump inquiry: Russians charged over US 2016 election tampering.* [Online]
Available at: http://www.bbc.co.uk/news/world-us-canada-43092085
[Accessed 17 02 2018].

BBC Entertainment and Arts, 2017. *BBC to help students identify 'fake news'.* [Online]
Available at: http://www.bbc.co.uk/news/entertainment-arts-42242630
[Accessed 12 01 2018].

BBC Middle East, 2016. *'Food crisis' hits 10,000 laid-off Indians in Saudi Arabia.* [Online]
Available at: http://www.bbc.co.uk/news/world-middle-east-36936666
[Accessed 18 01 2018].

BBC News, 2009. *I did not cause Rock run - Peston.* [Online]
Available at: http://news.bbc.co.uk/1/hi/uk_politics/7870240.stm
[Accessed 04 01 2018].

BBC News, 2013. *Burger King Twitter account 'hacked' with McDonald's logo.* [Online]
Available at: http://www.bbc.co.uk/news/world-us-canada-21500175
[Accessed 02 01 2018].

BBC News, 2016. *Internet trolls targeted with new legal guidelines.* [Online]
Available at: http://www.bbc.co.uk/news/uk-37601431
[Accessed 17 12 2017].

BBC News, 2017 (b). *San Francisco: Man arrested over 'Christmas terror plan'.* [Online]
Available at: http://www.bbc.co.uk/news/world-us-canada-42462463
[Accessed 23 12 2017].

BBC News, 2017. *Lazio fans give referee's cafe negative TripAdvisor reviews after controversial red card.* [Online]
Available at: http://www.bbc.co.uk/sport/football/42342987
[Accessed 15 12 2017].

BBC News, 2017. *Russia: The 'cloud' over the Trump White House.* [Online]
Available at: http://www.bbc.co.uk/news/world-us-canada-38966846
[Accessed 21 12 2017].

BBC News, 2018. *Akubra girl Dolly's bullying suicide shocks Australia.* [Online]

Available at: http://www.bbc.co.uk/news/world-australia-42631208
[Accessed 10 01 2018].

BBC News, 2018. *'Grooming alerts' call for social media.* [Online]
Available at: http://www.bbc.co.uk/news/uk-42855172
[Accessed 29 01 2018].

BBC News, 2018. *Hawaii missile alert: False alarm sparks panic in US state.* [Online]
Available at: http://www.bbc.co.uk/news/world-us-canada-42677604
[Accessed 14 01 2018].

BBC Radio 4, 2017. *Obama warns against irresponsible social media use.* [Online]
Available at: http://www.bbc.co.uk/news/world-us-canada-42491638
[Accessed 31 12 2017].

Beech, K., 2018. *This Manchester Hotel Had A Hilarious Response To A Bad TripAdvisor Review.* [Online]
Available at: https://lovinmanchester.com/feature/manchester-hotel-bites-back-at-bad-review
[Accessed 30 01 2018].

Big Brother Watch, 2018. *About Us.* [Online]
Available at: https://bigbrotherwatch.org.uk/about/
[Accessed 28 01 2018].

Blum, S. D., 2010. *My Word!: Plagiarism and College Culture.* s.l.:Cornell University Press.

Bowcott, O., Carter, H. & Clifton, H., 2011. *Facebook riot calls earn men four-year jail terms amid sentencing outcry.* [Online]
Available at: https://www.theguardian.com/uk/2011/aug/16/facebook-riot-calls-men-jailed
[Accessed 23 12 2017].

Bradley, D., 2017. *United Airlines faces social media backlash after forcibly removing passenger.* [Online]
Available at: https://www.prweek.com/article/1430176/united-airlines-faces-social-media-backlash-forcibly-removing-passenger
[Accessed 30 12 2017].

Brahmbhatt, M. & Dutta, A., 2008. *On SARS Type Economic Effects During Infectious Disease Outbreaks,* Washington, DC: World Bank.

BS 11200, 2014. *Crisis Management: Guidance and good practice.* 2014 ed. s.l.:British Standards Institute.

Burns, J., 2017. *Fake news: Universities offer tips on how to spot it.* [Online]
Available at: http://www.bbc.co.uk/news/education-41902914
[Accessed 12 01 2018].

Calfas, J., 2017. *Officer Who Forcibly Removed Passenger From United Airlines Flight Placed on Leave.* [Online]
Available at: http://time.com/4733652/united-airlines-chicago-passenger-officer-leave/
[Accessed 30 12 2017].

Callega, C., 2011. *Factory blaze takes hours to put out.* [Online]
Available at:
https://www.timesofmalta.com/articles/view/20110413/local/Factory-blaze-takes-hours-to-put-out.359696
[Accessed 21 12 2017].

Campbell, D., 2005. *I'm off.* [Online]
Available at:
https://www.theguardian.com/uk/2005/mar/13/football.deniscampbell
[Accessed 16 12 2017].

Campbell, D., 2017. *Facebook and Twitter 'harm young people's mental health.* [Online]

Available at:
https://www.theguardian.com/society/2017/may/19/popular-social-media-sites-harm-young-peoples-mental-health
[Accessed 03 12 2017].

Carsten, P., 2014. *China censors try to blunt Hong Kong protests, don't always succeed.* [Online]
Available at: https://www.reuters.com/article/us-hongkong-china-internet/china-censors-try-to-blunt-hong-kong-protests-dont-always-succeed-idUSKCN0HO1KV20140929
[Accessed 24 12 2017].

Casciani, D., 2018. *Ethan Stables: Bisexual terrorist who hated himself.* [Online]
Available at: http://www.bbc.co.uk/news/uk-42920765
[Accessed 07 02 2018].

CDC, 2004. *Preliminary Results from the World Trade Center Evacuation Study --- New York City, 2003.* [Online]
Available at:
https://www.cdc.gov/mmwr/preview/mmwrhtml/mm5335a3.htm
[Accessed 05 12 2017].

Cheng, Y. & Cameron, G., 2017. The status of social-mediated crisis management (SMCC) research. In: L. Austin & Y. Jin, eds. *Social Media and Crisis Communications.* NewYork, NY: Routledge.

Childline, 2016. *What children are telling us about bullying.* [Online]
Available at:
https://www.nspcc.org.uk/globalassets/documents/research-reports/what-children-are-telling-us-about-bullying-childline-bullying-report-2015-16.pdf
[Accessed 10 01 2018].

Childline, 2017. *What's online grooming.* [Online]
Available at: https://www.childline.org.uk/info-advice/bullying-abuse-safety/online-mobile-safety/online-grooming/
[Accessed 08 01 2017].

Choi, C. Q., 2011. *Twin Towers Forensic Investigation Helps Revise Building Codes, Despite Critics.* [Online]
Available at: https://www.scientificamerican.com/article/twin-towers-forensic-investigation-revise-building-codes/
[Accessed 05 12 2017].

CIA Fire and Security, 2016. *How many CCTV Cameras are there in the UK?.* [Online]
Available at: http://ciafireandsecurity.co.uk/2015/05/13/how-many-cctv-cameras-are-there-in-the-uk/
[Accessed 27 12 2017].

CNN Media, 2017. *How social media is helping Houston deal with Harvey floods.* [Online]
Available at: http://money.cnn.com/2017/08/28/media/harvey-rescues-social-media-facebook-twitter/index.html
[Accessed 11 01 2018].

CNN News, 2017. *Crackdown on texting & jaywalking.* [Online]
Available at: https://www.youtube.com/watch?v=RN1q9lHX1h8
[Accessed 27 11 2017].

Coates, S., 2018. *Social media forms told to crack down on grooming.* [Online]
Available at: https://www.thetimes.co.uk/article/social-media-firms-told-to-crack-down-ongrooming-3wt8v02sz
[Accessed 29 01 2018].

Cockram, D., 2015. *Comparative overview of the new British Standard for crisis management BS 11200 with NFPA 1600.* [Online]

Available at: https://www.regesterlarkin.com/wp-content/uploads/Comparative-overview-between-BS-11200-and-NFPA-1600.pdf
[Accessed 17 01 2018].

Cox, J., 2016. *Cops monitoring social media is much more than just collecting tweets.* [Online]
Available at: https://motherboard.vice.com/en_us/article/nz7q88/cops-monitoring-social-media-is-much-more-than-just-collecting-tweets
[Accessed 23 12 2017].

Critchell, M., 2016. *Poppy Appeal thief jailed for one year for stealing six collection tins from Southend businesses.* [Online]
Available at: http://www.echo-news.co.uk/news/14893530.Poppy_Appeal_thief_jailed_for_one_year_for_stealing_six_collection_tins_from_Southend_businesses/
[Accessed 04 09 2017].

Dawley, S., 2016. *Social Media Crisis Management: How to Prepare and Execute a Plan.* [Online]
Available at: https://blog.hootsuite.com/social-media-crisis-management/
[Accessed 02 02 2018].

De Castella, T. & McClatchey, C., 2011. *UK riots: What turns people into looters?.* [Online]
Available at: http://www.bbc.co.uk/news/magazine-14463452
[Accessed 23 12 2017].

Delaney, J., 2017. *Crisis management case study: United Airlines.* [Online]
Available at: http://www.netimperative.com/2017/05/crisis-management-case-study-united-airlines/
[Accessed 22 12 2017].

Digital EYE, 2015. *Three Social Media Posting Mistakes That Can Cause a PR Disaster.* [Online]
Available at: http://www.digitaleyemedia.com/social-media/three-social-media-posting-mistakes-that-can-cause-a-pr-disaster
[Accessed 10 01 2018].

Dolman Law Group, 2016. *Can social media use harm your personal injury claim?.* [Online]
Available at: https://www.dolmanlaw.com/can-social-media-use-harm-personal-injury-claim/
[Accessed 27 11 2017].

Donnelly, C., 2010. *PR triathlete uses Twitter to contact rescuers.* [Online]
Available at: https://www.prweek.com/article/1266925/pr-triathlete-uses-twitter-contact-rescuers
[Accessed 18 01 2018].

Dwyer, J., 2005. *Vast archives yields new view of 9/11.* [Online]
Available at:
http://www.nytimes.com/2005/08/13/nyregion/nyregionspecial3/vast-archive-yields-new-view-of-911.html
[Accessed 06 12 2017].

Edwards, R., 2009. *British entrepreneur Rob Williams dies on skiing holiday in tragedy played out on Twitter.* [Online]
Available at:
http://www.telegraph.co.uk/technology/twitter/4933281/British-entrepreneur-Rob-Williams-dies-on-skiing-holiday-in-tragedy-played-out-on-Twitter.html
[Accessed 18 01 2018].

Environics Communications Inc, 2016. *CRISIS MANAGEMENT IN A SOCIAL MEDIA WORLD.* [Online]
Available at: http://www.environicsdc.com/guides/crisis-

managementrisis-management-in-a-social-media-world
[Accessed 30 01 2018].

ESRC, 2015. *Security, terrorism and social media.* [Online]
Available at: http://www.esrc.ac.uk/news-events-and-publications/evidence-briefings/security-terrorism-and-social-media/
[Accessed 01 02 2018].

EU 261, 2004. *Establishing common rules on compensation and assistance to passengers in the event of denied boarding and of cancellation or long delay of flights.* [Online]
Available at: http://eur-lex.europa.eu/legal-content/EN/ALL/?uri=celex%3A32004R0261
[Accessed 31 12 2017].

Evac Chair, 2001. *Saving a life in an efficient manner, is the core of our product development - The story of one man's escape from the World Trade Center on 9/11/2001.* [Online]
Available at: http://www.evac-chair.com/911/
[Accessed 05 12 2017].

Facebook, 2018. *https://www.facebook.com/ThisIsMustard/.* [Online]
[Accessed 15 01 2018].

Facebook, 2018. *Safety Check.* [Online]
Available at: https://www.facebook.com/help/695378390556779
[Accessed 11 01 2018].

Fadilpašić, S., 2015. *Millennials realize social media mistakes could damage their career.* [Online]
Available at: https://betanews.com/2016/05/25/social-media-career-damage/
[Accessed 01 12 2017].

Feeney, C., 2014. The Devastating Effect of the SARS Pandemic on the Tourist Industry. In: R. Clark, ed. *In Hindsight - a compendium of business continuity case studies.* Cambridge, UK: ITGP.

Finegan, S., 2013. *How Social Media can play havoc with your business continuity.* [Online]
Available at:
www.manchester.gov.uk/downloads/download/5713/social_media_and_business_continuity
[Accessed 12 06 2015].

Fishwick, B., 2016. *WATCH: Charity tin thief caught on CCTV in Portsmouth pub.* [Online]
Available at: http://www.portsmouth.co.uk/news/crime/watch-charity-tin-thief-caught-on-cctv-in-portsmouth-pub-1-7218536
[Accessed 04 09 2017].

Flock, E., 2011. *Kawasaki disease diagnosed on Facebook, helping to save Leo Kogan's life.* [Online]
Available at:
https://www.washingtonpost.com/blogs/blogpost/post/kawasaki-disease-diagnosed-on-facebook--saving-leo-kogans-life/2011/07/15/gIQAtkOKGI_blog.html?utm_term=.5114ce5cb83c
[Accessed 18 01 2018].

Football Italia Staff, 2017. *Lazio fans mock Giacomelli.* [Online]
Available at: https://www.football-italia.net/114184/lazio-fans-mock-giacomelli
[Accessed 17 12 2017].

Future Learn, 2018. *Making Sense of Data in the Media.* [Online]
Available at: https://www.futurelearn.com/courses/media-data
[Accessed 12 01 2018].

Gilmer, M., 2017. *Social media proves to be a positive force in flooded Texas.* [Online]
Available at: http://mashable.com/2017/08/29/social-media-harvey-rescues-force-for-good/#imEgDyhlsOqx
[Accessed 11 01 2018].

Glendinning, L., 2001. *9/11 survivors put off evacuation to shut down computers, study finds.* [Online]
Available at:
https://www.theguardian.com/world/2008/sep/09/september11.usa
[Accessed 05 12 2017].

Gov UK, 2012. *Smart Tips for Category 1 Responders Using Social Media in Emergency Management.* [Online]
Available at:
https://www.gov.uk/government/uploads/system/uploads/attachment_data/file/85946/Using-social-media-in-emergencies-smart-tips.pdf
[Accessed 03 02 2018].

Green, N., 2015(b). *Teaching Social Media in Our Schools.* [Online]
[Accessed 08 01 2018].

Greenslade, R., 2015. *The D-notice system: a typically British fudge that has survived a century.* [Online]
Available at: https://www.theguardian.com/media/2015/jul/31/d-notice-system-state-media-press-freedom
[Accessed 24 12 2017].

Guardian Sport, 2016. *Referee 'shot dead by player he sent off' during amateur match in Argentina.* [Online]
Available at: https://www.theguardian.com/football/2016/feb/16/referee-shot-dead-by-player-sent-off-argentina
[Accessed 16 12 2017].

Halliday, J., 2011. *UK riots 'made worse' by rolling news, BBM, Twitter and Facebook.* [Online]
Available at: https://www.theguardian.com/media/2012/mar/28/uk-riots-twitter-facebook
[Accessed 24 12 2017].

Heilweil, R., 2017. *Harvard Rescinds Admissions To 10 Students For Offensive Facebook Memes.* [Online]
Available at:
https://www.forbes.com/sites/rebeccaheilweil1/2017/06/05/harvard-rescinds-10-admissions-offer-for-offensive-facebook-memes-ollowing-commencement-speaker-zuckerberg/#2ba2e56f3dbd
[Accessed 09 01 2018].

Heward, E., 2017. *Donors asked not to visit blood banks without an appointment in wake of Manchester terror attack.* [Online]
Available at: http://www.manchestereveningnews.co.uk/news/greater-manchester-news/manchester-blood-banks-terror-attack-13077365
[Accessed 11 01 2018].

Hicks, J., 2006. *PR Crisis Management - Tell It All, Tell It Fast And Tell The Truth.* [Online]
Available at: http://ezinearticles.com/?PR-Crisis-Management---Tell-It-All,-Tell-It-Fast-And-Tell-The-Truth&id=204295
[Accessed 22 05 2015].

Hobson, J., 2016. *9/11 Survivor Brian Clark Reflects On His Escape, 15 Years Later.* [Online]
Available at: http://www.wbur.org/hereandnow/2016/09/07/911-survivor-brian-clark
[Accessed 08 12 2017].

Hootsuite, 2018. *10 Types of Social Media and How Each Can Benefit Your Business.* [Online]

Available at: https://blog.hootsuite.com/types-of-social-media/
[Accessed 29 01 2018].

Hootsuite, 2018. *Social is our DNA.* [Online]
Available at: https://hootsuite.com/en-gb/about#
[Accessed 29 01 2018].

Huffington Post, 2010. *Injured Biker Leigh Fazzina Rescued By Twitter.*
[Online]
Available at: https://www.huffingtonpost.com/2010/08/03/leigh-fazzina-injured-bik_n_669175.html
[Accessed 18 01 2018].

James, P., 2014. *Umbrella Revolution* [Interview] (03 10 2014).

JustGiving, 2017. *We've raised £2,587,667 to support families of those killed and injured in the Manchester Arena attack.* [Online]
Available at:
https://www.justgiving.com/crowdfunding/westandtogethermanchester
[Accessed 11 01 2018].

Kapko, M., 2014. *Is Social Media Reviving or Killing Our Classrooms?.*
[Online]
Available at: https://www.cio.com/article/2604686/social-media/is-social-media-reviving-or-killing-our-classrooms.html
[Accessed 09 01 2018].

Kapko, M., 2014. *Is Social Media Reviving or Killing Our Classrooms?.*
[Online]
Available at: https://www.cio.com/article/2604686/social-media/is-social-media-reviving-or-killing-our-classrooms.html
[Accessed 12 01 2018].

Kassam, A., 2014. *Can instant messaging damage your health? Doctor warns of 'WhatsAppitis'.* [Online]
Available at:

https://www.theguardian.com/technology/2014/mar/26/can-instant-messaging-damage-health-doctor-warns-whatsappitis
[Accessed 27 11 2017].

Kean, T. et al., 2004. *The 9/11 Commisision Report,* s.l.: US Government.

Kennedy, E., 2017. *'Just a joke': Students' social media threats are disrupting schools.* [Online]
Available at: http://www.pnj.com/story/news/crime/2017/10/15/how-students-social-media-threats-disrupting-schools-involving-police/753349001/
[Accessed 04 01 2018].

Koler, R., 2011. *Stairwell "A".* [Online]
Available at: http://nymag.com/news/9-11/10th-anniversary/stairwell-a/
[Accessed 08 12 2017].

Kwong, R., 2014. *China censors Hong Kong's 'Umbrella Revolution'.* [Online]
Available at: http://www.ejinsight.com/20140930-hong-kong-occupy-central-china-censorship/
[Accessed 23 12 2017].

Mail Online, 2011. *Big Brother is DEFINITELY watching you: Shocking study reveals UK has one CCTV for every 32 people.* [Online]
Available at: http://www.dailymail.co.uk/news/article-1362493/One-CCTV-camera-32-people-Big-Brother-Britain.html
[Accessed 27 12 2017].

Mallinson, H., 2016. *A plane mistake! British Airways accidentally recommends its Facebook followers to fly with big rivals Virgin Atlantic in embarrassing social media mix-up.* [Online]
Available at: http://www.dailymail.co.uk/travel/travel_news/article-3862042/A-plane-mistake-British-Airways-accidentally-recommends-

Facebook-followers-fly-big-rivals-Virgin-Atlantic-embarrassing-social-media-mix-up.html
[Accessed 02 01 2018].

Marsh, P., 2017. *Abuse causing amateur football referees to quit.*
[Online]
Available at: http://www.bbc.co.uk/news/uk-wales-41585962
[Accessed 15 12 2017].

McVeigh, K. & Rankin, J., 2017. *British public helps to raise £50m in 22 days for east Africa hunger crisis.* [Online]
Available at: https://www.theguardian.com/global-development/2017/apr/06/british-public-donates-72m-east-africa-yemen-hunger-disasters-emergency-committee
[Accessed 12 12 2017].

Mercy Corps, 2015. *QUICK FACTS: WHAT YOU NEED TO KNOW ABOUT THE NEPAL EARTHQUAKE.* [Online]
Available at: https://www.mercycorps.org/articles/nepal/quick-facts-what-you-need-know-about-nepal-earthquake
[Accessed 11 01 2018].

Messanger Garrett, M., 2017. *During a Crisis, How Should Brands Behave on Social Media?.* [Online]
Available at: https://www.linkedin.com/pulse/during-crisis-how-should-brands-behave-social-media-michelle/
[Accessed 11 01 2018].

Millar, J., 2016. *WATCH: Fury as 'SCUMBAG' filmed stealing poppy tin from restaurant IN FRONT of diners.* [Online]
Available at: http://www.express.co.uk/news/uk/730003/poppy-tin-donation-theft-mangetout-southend-british-legion
[Accessed 04 09 2017].

Mitchell, E. S., 2013. *PR Fail: Food Website Exploits Boston Tragedy.* [Online]
Available at: http://www.adweek.com/digital/pr-fail-food-website-exploits-boston-tragedy/
[Accessed 12 01 2018].

Mizen, L., 2018. *Student at Marjory Stoneman Douglas High* [Interview] (17 02 2018).

NBC News, 2008. *Voices will bring relics to life at 9/11 museum.* [Online]
Available at: http://www.nbcnews.com/id/26644318/ns/us_news-9_11_seven_years_later/t/voices-will-bring-relics-life-museum/#.WifNpkpl-Uk
[Accessed 06 12 2017].

NDTV, 2016. *Over 10,000 Indians Facing Food Scarcity In Saudi Arabia, Says Sushma Swaraj.* [Online]
Available at: https://www.ndtv.com/indians-abroad/over-10-000-indians-facing-food-scarcity-in-saudi-arabia-says-sushma-swaraj-1438302
[Accessed 18 01 2018].

NHS, 2018. *Kawasaki Disease.* [Online]
Available at: https://www.nhs.uk/conditions/Kawasaki-disease/
[Accessed 18 01 2018].

Noble, M., 2017. *Thief Trackers: Series 3, Episode 1,* Southend-on-Sea: Crook Productions for the BBC.

NSPCC - London, 2016. *What children are telling us about bullying.* [Online]
Available at: Bullying affects academic performance and is linked to mental and physical health problems. In a quarter of counselling sessions about bullying, children also talked about mental health and

wellbeing issues.
[Accessed 10 01 2018].

O'Carrol, K., 2011. *Police beam images of wanted riot suspects on to giant screens.* [Online]
Available at: https://www.theguardian.com/uk/2011/aug/12/police-wanted-riot-suspects-looter
[Accessed 24 12 2017].

Oliver, T., 2015. *The truth behind Rex Secco's £34million transfer move to Arsenal.* [Online]
Available at: http://metro.co.uk/2015/09/07/the-truth-behind-rex-seccos-34million-transfer-move-to-arsenal-5380023/
[Accessed 20 12 2017].

Oregan Sports, 2017. *Adidas apologizes following poorly worded Boston Marathon email that provoked social media backlash.* [Online]
Available at:
http://www.oregonlive.com/sports/index.ssf/2017/04/adidas_boston_marathon_ad_fail.html
[Accessed 11 01 2018].

Pan, J., 2012. *Student Threatens School Shooting Spree on Reddit, Gets Arrested [VIDEO].* [Online]
Available at: http://mashable.com/2012/03/13/alexander-song-reddit/#Rjh9qeEsd5qs
[Accessed 09 01 2018].

Perkins, B., 2017. *United Airlines' mishandling of Flight 3411 provides powerful lessons on how to avoid creating a crisis.* [Online]
Available at: https://www.computerworld.com/article/3193764/it-management/lessons-from-a-flight-gone-wrong.html
[Accessed 31 12 2017].

Praetorius, D., 2012. *How Social Media Would Have Changed New York on 9/11.* [Online]
Available at: https://www.huffingtonpost.com/dean-praetorius/social-media-9-11-new-york_b_1872764.html
[Accessed 05 12 2017].

Quinn, B., 2014. *TripAdvisor couple fined £100 by hotel for bad review.* [Online]
Available at: https://www.theguardian.com/uk-news/2014/nov/19/tripadvisor-couple-bad-hotel-review-charged-blackpool-broadway
[Accessed 10 01 2018].

Quiñonero Candela, J., 2017. *Managing Your Identity on Facebook with Face Recognition Technology.* [Online]
Available at: https://newsroom.fb.com/news/2017/12/managing-your-identity-on-facebook-with-face-recognition-technology/
[Accessed 30 12 2017].

Rafferty, J. & Pletcher, K., 2011. *Japan earthquake and tsunami of 2011.* [Online]
Available at: https://www.britannica.com/event/Japan-earthquake-and-tsunami-of-2011
[Accessed 28 01 2018].

Read, S., 2017. *One million homes still at risk from deadly tumble dryers.* [Online]
Available at: http://www.bbc.co.uk/news/business-your-money-41819779
[Accessed 30 01 2018].

Reuters, 2014. *China blocks BBC website as Hong Kong tensions rise.* [Online]
Available at: https://www.reuters.com/article/us-china-censorship/china-blocks-bbc-website-as-hong-kong-tensions-rise-

idUSKCN0I505S20141016
[Accessed 24 12 2017].

Rhodan, M., 2017. *'Please Send Help.' Hurricane Harvey Victims Turn to Twitter and Facebook.* [Online]
Available at: http://time.com/4921961/hurricane-harvey-twitter-facebook-social-media/
[Accessed 11 01 2018].

Ricketts, S., 2013. *How the Boston Marathon explosions reveal the two sides of Twitter.* [Online]
Available at:
https://www.theguardian.com/commentisfree/2013/apr/16/boston-marathon-explosions-reveal-twitter
[Accessed 11 01 2018].

Rogers, C., 2017. *Teachers want social media ethics taught in schools.* [Online]
Available at: http://edtechnology.co.uk/Article/teachers-want-social-media-ethics-taught-in-schools
[Accessed 08 01 2018].

Ryan, L., 2017. *https://www.forbes.com/sites/lizryan/2017/05/07/five-social-media-mistakes-that-will-hurt-your-job-search/#1c62fb0cd39d.* [Online]
Available at: https://www.forbes.com/sites/lizryan/2017/05/07/five-social-media-mistakes-that-will-hurt-your-job-search/#1c62fb0cd39d
[Accessed 01 12 2017].

Savitch, H., 2008. *Cities in a time of terror: space, territory, and local resilience.* New York: M.E Sharpe Inc.

Savitch, H., 2008. *Cities in a time of terror: space, territory, and local resilience..* New York, NY: M.E Sharpe Inc..

Schamis, I., 2018. *BBC Breakfast* [Interview] (16 02 2018).

Sharp, M., 2015. *Beware the smartphone zombies blindly wandering around Hong Kong.* [Online]
Available at:
http://www.scmp.com/lifestyle/technology/article/1725001/smartphone-zombies-are-putting-your-life-and-theirs-danger
[Accessed 04 12 2017].

Shelton, J., 2017. *The Biggest Corporate Social Media Fails And Disasters Of 2017.* [Online]
Available at: https://www.ranker.com/list/corporate-social-media-fails-2017/jacob-shelton
[Accessed 11 01 2018].

Silverman, C., 2016. *This Analysis Shows How Viral Fake Election News Stories Outperformed Real News On Facebook.* [Online]
Available at: https://www.buzzfeed.com/craigsilverman/viral-fake-election-news-outperformed-real-news-on-facebook?utm_term=.ecM5LQ6Ye#.hiPLIZo1a
[Accessed 20 12 2017].

Solon, O., 2016. *Facebook says likely Russia-based group paid for political ads during US election.* [Online]
Available at:
https://www.theguardian.com/technology/2017/sep/06/facebook-political-ads-russia-us-election-trump-clinton
[Accessed 20 12 2017].

Spielman, F., 2017. *Two of the aviation cops who dragged doctor off United flight fired.* [Online]
Available at: https://chicago.suntimes.com/chicago-politics/aviation-cops-who-dragged-doctor-off-united-flight-have-been-fired/
[Accessed 31 12 2017].

Stewart, J., 2017. *The boycott that wasn't: United weathered a media firestorm.* [Online]

Available at: https://www.nytimes.com/2017/07/27/business/how-united-weathered-a-firestorm.html
[Accessed 09 01 2018].

Swaine, J., 2017. *New fake news dilemma: sites publish real scoops amid mess of false reports.* [Online]
Available at: https://www.theguardian.com/media/2017/may/16/fake-news-sites-reports-facts-louise-mensch
[Accessed 20 12 2017].

Swallow, E., 2017. *How Recruiters Use Social Networks to Screen Candidates.* [Online]
Available at: http://mashable.com/2011/10/23/how-recruiters-use-social-networks-to-screen-candidates-infographic/#5gsmVKlhdaqn
[Accessed 12 01 2017].

Taras, V., 2017. *How Social Media Encourages Plagiarism (and Six Ways You Can Fight It).* [Online]
Available at: https://www.edsurge.com/news/2017-11-13-how-social-media-encourages-plagiarism-and-six-ways-you-can-fight-it
[Accessed 12 01 2018].

Taylor, D., 2017. *Teenager jailed for trolling footballer Andy Woodward about abuse.* [Online]
Available at: https://www.theguardian.com/uk-news/2017/dec/15/teenager-jailed-for-trolling-footballer-andy-woodward-about-abuse
[Accessed 17 12 2017].

Taylor, J., 2018. *Facebook moderator: I had to be prepared to see anything.* [Online]
Available at: http://www.bbc.co.uk/news/technology-42920554
[Accessed 08 02 2018].

Telegraph, 2015. *Five internet trolls a day convicted in UK as figures show ten-fold increase.* [Online]
Available at: http://www.telegraph.co.uk/news/uknews/law-and-order/11627180/Five-internet-trolls-a-day-convicted-in-UK-as-figures-show-ten-fold-increase.html
[Accessed 17 12 2017].

TripAdvisor, 2018. *Broadway Hotel.* [Online]
Available at: https://www.tripadvisor.co.uk/Hotel_Review-g186332-d554701-Reviews-Broadway_Hotel-Blackpool_Lancashire_England.html
[Accessed 10 01 2018].

TripAdvisor, 2018. *Disapponted.* [Online]
Available at: https://www.tripadvisor.co.uk/ShowUserReviews-g1022653-d10474568-r553589999-Mustard-Sale_Trafford_Greater_Manchester_England.html
[Accessed 15 01 2018].

Twitter, 2015. *Arsenal is said to be in the final stages of securing a deal for 16 year old Rex Secco, for a fee believed to be £34m.* [Online]
Available at:
https://twitter.com/LaughingFooty/status/640570044620128257?ref_src=twsrc%5Etfw&ref_url=http%3A%2F%2Fwww.90min.com%2Fposts%2F2533710-who-is-rex-secco-fake-football-player-trends-on-twitter-after-arsenal-signing
[Accessed 20 12 2017].

Twitter, 2017. *#VTNEW Due to the emergency services dealing with an incident between Milton Keynes Central and Watford Junction all lines are blocked..* [Online]
Available at:
https://twitter.com/VirginTrains/status/942745006472822784
[Accessed 18 12 2017].

Twitter, 2017. *United CEO response to United Express Flight 3411..* [Online]
Available at:
https://twitter.com/search?q=%40united%20united%20CEO%20respon
se%20to%20UNited%20express%20flight%203411&src=typd
[Accessed 30 12 2017].

Twitter, 2018. *Jeremy HUnt.* [Online]
Available at:
https://twitter.com/Jeremy_Hunt/status/950461803997384704?ref_src=
twsrc%5Egoogle%7Ctwcamp%5Eserp%7Ctwgr%5Etweet
[Accessed 09 01 2018].

UK Cabinet Office, 2017. *National Risk Register of Civil Emergencies – 2017 Edition.* [Online]
Available at: https://www.gov.uk/government/publications/national-risk-register-of-civil-emergencies-2017-edition
[Accessed 30 01 2018].

Vickers, H., 2017. *Social media disrupts 11 days' teaching time a year.* [Online]
Available at: http://edtechnology.co.uk/Article/social-media-disrupts-11-days-teaching-time-a-year
[Accessed 09 01 2018].

Volkswagon, 2014. *MCL cinema Hong Kong Mobile phone car crash advertising effective.* [Online]
Available at: https://www.youtube.com/watch?v=5Gtio4V1L3o
[Accessed 27 11 2017].

Vulliamy, E., 2001. *Anger of survivors told to stay inside blazing towers.* [Online]
Available at:
https://www.theguardian.com/world/2001/sep/16/september11.usa3
[Accessed 05 12 2017].

Wakefield, J., 2017. *The man who can't face the internet.* [Online]
Available at: http://www.bbc.co.uk/news/technology-42265053
[Accessed 30 12 2017].

Wallop, H., 2011. *Japan earthquake: how Twitter and Facebook helped.* [Online]
Available at:
http://www.telegraph.co.uk/technology/twitter/8379101/Japan-earthquake-how-Twitter-and-Facebook-helped.html
[Accessed 28 01 2018].

Were, D. K., 2013. *How Kenya turned to social media after mall attack.* [Online]
Available at: http://edition.cnn.com/2013/09/25/opinion/kenya-social-media-attack/index.html
[Accessed 12 12 2017].

Which, 2017. *Update: it's unacceptable that Whirlpool is still failing consumers.* [Online]
Available at: https://conversation.which.co.uk/home-energy/whirlpool-fire-risk-tumble-dryers-one-year-on/
[Accessed 30 01 2018].

Whitman, H., 2016. *COULD CYBERBULLYING BE CAUSING A RISE IN ABSENTEEISM?.* [Online]
Available at: http://www.theedadvocate.org/cyberbullying-causing-rise-absenteeism/
[Accessed 10 01 2018].

Whitten, S., 2015. *Rumors and misinformation circulate on social media following Paris attacks.* [Online]
Available at: https://www.cnbc.com/2015/11/14/rumors-and-misinformation-circulate-on-social-media-following-paris-attacks.html
[Accessed 07 12 2017].

Williams, O., 2011. *London Riots: Twitter That Caused Them?*. [Online]
Available at: http://www.huffingtonpost.co.uk/2011/08/08/london-riots-twitter-that_n_920791.html
[Accessed 23 12 2017].

Zoltick, L., 2018. *The Good, Bad, and In-Between of Social Media In Crisis Situations.* [Online]
Available at: https://isl.co/2014/10/the-good-bad-and-in-between-of-social-media-in-crisis-situations/
[Accessed 17 01 2018].

Zoppo, A., 2017. *McDonald's Investigating Anti-Trump Tweet Sent From Company Account.* [Online]
Available at: https://www.nbcnews.com/news/us-news/mcdonald-s-investigating-anti-trump-tweet-sent-company-account-n734411
[Accessed 11 01 2018].

15. Open Government License

32094218R00132

Printed in Great Britain
by Amazon